INSIDE YOUR HEAVEN

Inspiring Stories of the Afterlife

April Natale

Dedication

For my two beautiful children, Stephen and Mariah,

May you find the courage within yourselves to conquer the world with love and light by listening to that still small voice within and by honoring the gentle guidance from our Angels of heaven. Trust your soul's journey in this life; continue to find me and each other in this lifetime and the next. Always be there for one another; always trust your Intuition and your gifts: always listen to your Angels!

I'll Always Love you both,
from this life into the next, Mom

"The soul is invisible.

An angel is invisible.

The wind is invisible.

Thoughts are invisible.

And yet, with sensitivity,

you can see the soul,

you can guess the angel,

you can feel the wind,

you can change the world

with only a few thoughts."

– Paulo Coelho

Table of Contents:

Preface

The angels spoke to April when she was a child. She had been badly abused and their presence gave her solace. She didn't know at such a vulnerable age that she was actually honing in on her gifts, and not knowing that gave her an overwhelming feeling of anxiety as well as a sense of responsibility.

It wasn't until she lost several loved ones that she began to wonder what it was like inside of heaven. And that constant, nagging thought is what finally got her to surrender and accept her ability to connect with those in the afterlife.

In *Inside Your Heaven, Inspiring Stories From the Afterlife,* April shares her journey from abused child to self-actualized adult and the experiences in her life that led her to accept her gifts as well as stories that validated her experience.

By the end of the book, the reader will absolutely believe that it is possible to connect with loved ones in heaven and how a psychic medium can help.

And for those who fear talking to angels, April will alleviate all fears as she shares what a gift it is and how it can be used for good in the world!

CHAPTER ONE:

Awakening

Ever since I was a little girl, I would sit outside and look up at the crystal blue sky and just wonder what it was like to be inside Heaven. I was always knocking on Heaven's door. I felt a very strong connection to "the other side." It felt peaceful to me, and natural, to be so curious about where we come from and how we got here. I always had this inner voice telling me, "remember why you came here, and we will be here to guide you along the way."

Little did I know then that I was able to peek inside heaven just by connecting with Spirit and passed loved ones on the other side. The veil is very thin, thinner than we can ever imagine. Our loved ones truly are not locked up in Heaven: they're right here, almost as if just in the next room. I didn't always know that I was a Psychic Medium, but, at the same time, I always did know, because my gift was a part of my heart and soul. To be honest, that gift scared me at times because of the things I would see, hear, and feel. I felt cursed when I would know certain people were going to die—and then they would. It wasn't until my early adulthood that it took such a spiritual awakening for me to finally surrender and follow my soul's path and purpose. I had to stop caring what other people thought about me so that I could do what God wants me to do here on earth.

I'd have to say, the tragic loss of my step dad John really knocked me down and, at the same time, made me realize the strength of my abilities. Some people might call what I experienced a mental breakdown, but some would call it a spiritual awakening. I'd say my human self was having a breakdown—but my soul was on fire, awakening every fiber within me to do this type of service. I didn't tell anyone how strong my abilities were, because I didn't really understand them myself.

"Who looks outside, dreams; who looks inside, awakes."
– Carl Jung

I was sitting outside one day with my step dad, and John said to me, "April, I worry about your mother and how she will be if my cancer treatments don't go well." I told him that if anything happened to him, he could come to me, and I would let mom know what he wanted me to tell her. I told him I would do anything he would need me to say or do. I explained to him I "sort of" have this gift, an ability to connect with people on the other side—so he could just let me know what he needed me to do. He kind of looked at me gently and in a funny manner, but I know deep down he believed me.

Unfortunately, after losing his battle to cancer, within days my step dad came to me in my sleep and poked my foot! I jolted awake. I knew it was him. I was so distraught and grief-stricken by his death that I said to him, "You didn't make it; you passed from cancer." I told him, "Right now, I'm really sick to my stomach over your passing: I have to sleep. I'm not eating. None of this is making sense. You have to come to me in my dreams." I felt like I was in between two worlds. I know he heard me, because a few days later, he came to me in a dream just like I requested.

In that dream, I walked into a big dining room, and he was sitting at a table filled with people I didn't know. He wasn't skinny anymore, being able to eat once again. The only person I recognized was my mom sitting next to him, and she was rubbing and rubbing the right side of his neck where the radiation had been applied. My mom was feeding him, and he looked so happy and free! Then, in the vision, my sister walked up to me crying about an unborn baby girl. She also indicated our step dad was no longer acting like he was on hospice. I told her, "let's take him outside for sunlight and fresh air." I know that was the part of me that tried for control when he was alive and struggling with his cancer; then as soon as I walked up to him I woke up! I remember him looking at me so confused about what I hoped to control, because truly, God is in control—and that was part of the lesson I needed to learn surrounding his death.

The next day I texted my mom. I told her about my dream, and she said, "Wow, that's amazing: when he and I used to watch TV, I used to rub and rub his neck on his radiation spot, and I tried my hardest to make him feel better, because he had a lot of pain and numbness on that side."

I thought to myself: how could I possibly know this intimate detail between the two of them? I also relayed to my mom that my sister was crying in the dream, something about a baby girl, but, to be honest, I sensed she needed to do something medically first. I felt my step dad was giving me the opportunity to warn her that she will face some major health challenges, but that she would be all right in the end.

That was a powerful visitation. That's when I really knew just how gifted I was and how loved ones could come to me from Heaven to relay messages to their loved ones!

Within a few months, my sister went to her obstetrician in hopes of having another child. She had two boys already, so she was hoping for a girl, yet she didn't tell anyone she was trying to conceive. Shortly after, she found out after her pap smear result that she had early stages of cervical cancer. I then told her about my first visitation and dream with our step dad. I told her he revealed she would face medical challenges, but that she would recover just fine! My sister is set to have a full hysterectomy soon, and is considering the surrogacy route. Please send all your positive thoughts and healing vibes to her and her loving family.

I write this book for a few reasons: one major one being I believe our loved ones are not locked up in Heaven; St. Peter doesn't just lock the gates upon arrival and hide away the key. Our loved ones are right here with us , joining us on our car rides to work in the morning, and on the couch at night watching our regular night time shows. What lives on is the love and light that emanates from them. I can tell they are off doing other things and serving in more than one place at a time, like the way the sun rays touch down on earth in every state and every continent they too are rays of light.

Our loved ones do not change on the other side; they still have their same personalities, yet they are more enlightened. What they learn here is what they take with them and that determines their levels of consciousness, and yet on the other side, they will have more opportunities to learn and grow. We come here in "Soul-Groups" and some are here to play "good guys" and some "bad guys" in this school of life. Here on earth, we are at school, and, once we finish our life's lessons and serve our life's path and purposes, our Soul's Contract is up for this lifetime, and then we go home: home to the next level of consciousness on the other side which we often call Heaven.

I assure you, I'm also not here to change your views on life or your religious beliefs. I'm just here as another messenger of my generation, to share my experiences. I'm no different than the messengers before with these same gifts. I just have cooler clothes and more resources! I believe in all religious groups that contain beautiful messages from wonderful teachers and saints, but I also believe all the wisdom comes from One source: there is only one God, a forgiving and loving God, who allows endless opportunities and many "lifetimes" for us to gain the ultimate level of consciousness.

Basically, our journey is like that in Mario Land—where one must go through certain levels to get to the highest level, usually at the top of the castle. I don't believe in Hell; I believe in certain levels of consciousness in Heaven. I feel God gives us endless opportunities to advance. I know I won't want to hang out with low level energies in the next life. I will want to gain all I can in this life, so that I can sit in the upper levels of Heaven next to Mother Mary and Mother Teresa to ask them about their real true life stories. I want to meet Selena and Princess Diana; they were given such a beautiful platform in this life to do great things for our world by spreading love through music and charity. I want to tell Whitney Houston her healing voice helped me. I suspect these gifted artists somehow channel Angels from Heaven. I'm fascinated by Paul's McCartney's account of his mother Mary visiting him from Heaven—telling him to just "let it be"—a visitation which of course led to the famous Beatles' song.

> *"When I find myself in times of trouble, Mother Mary comes to me, Speaking words of wisdom; Let it be..."*

I want people like myself to no longer fear their abilities to connect with the other side, to no longer be so afraid as to need self-medication to compensate for feeling like you don't belong here anymore. Reader, you too, have gifts and are here to walk this earth as a lightworker.

I want people to know where or who they can go to for the spiritual help they need to grow. We have a mind, body, and soul, and, oftentimes, we are so caught up with the trappings of our society that we leave out the most important thing: the inner work that comes from the soul. We are fed so much superficial material from our society, including commercial ads for quick fix medications, but rarely do we seek real guidance for spiritual work.

I'm hoping this book offers just the right dose of spirituality that you need, along with some genuine guidance to help you through whatever you must endure.

"No pain that we suffer, no trial that we experience is wasted. It ministers to our education, to the development of such qualities as patience, faith, fortitude and humility. All that we suffer and all that we endure, especially when we endure it patiently, builds up our characters, purifies our hearts, expands our souls, and makes us more tender and charitable, more worthy to be called the children of God..."
– Orson F. Whitney

CHAPTER TWO:

Angels in Disguise That Evolve Your Soul

So, let me tell you a little bit about my childhood.

I go by April Natale to help you all from butchering and spelling my very Italian last name. I shortened it for you all to save you some time. Natale means Christmas in Italian: my Mom must have had a hunch that I was going to be just like good old Saint Nicholas and share my gifts with the world! (I was also her fourth girl, so I guess she must have run out of options for names.)

I was born (yes of course!) in April, of 1985 on Sayre Street in the Galewood area of Chicago, with a pretty big abnormal family, I'd say. I had a really good mother and a very funny loving grandmother, who also helped raise me. I grew up watching my mother handle any obstacle life threw at her. I'm sure she cried herself to sleep many nights, but she still got up every morning and did an amazing job raising us. My mom worked a lot downtown in our beautiful city. We lived within walking distance of the train that she would catch every morning. However, I had a very abusive father—a man who had 14 children total with two other women including my mom. Thankfully the other mothers were so very loving to me and my siblings.

My dad, well, he never really had a job. The only thing I remember was the construction trucks he had from some concrete work he did here and there. For the most part he would take my mom's hardworking money and gamble it away or spend it on his other children. Most of the time we sensed he hated us kids for no reason at all, as he repeated the same cycle he grew up with—instead of healing himself and choosing to do better.

His father also had multiple children in a few marriages, and he did the same thing to his kids, and his mom was with multiple men and did not show my dad the love he needed growing up.

I've been told that my dad's grandma was a healer like me and very loving. People would go to her for healing, and supposedly, she had psychic mediumship gifts as well. So, where this all went wrong was with them and the way they failed in how they chose to use their free will. We would go to visit his side of the family, usually by my dad's mom's house: Nana we would call her. They would put us kids in the basement and pop in a Disney movie for all of my siblings and cousins to watch while they were upstairs smoking heavily and playing cards at the kitchen table. If my siblings and I ever slept over at Nana's, we were often told to shut up and eat our cereal in the morning, and if not, my Nana would hit us over our heads with the box. Not a lot of good memories there! Although I did have a great time with my cousins and half siblings (mocking our Nana most of the time).

I did spend a lot of time with my siblings outside playing and laughing, riding bikes and even climbing trees. On the weekends I was always having sleepovers at my friend's house or spending nights with our mom's side at Aunt Gigi's, or at Grandma Honey's house; they were always our much needed safe haven. At Aunt Gigi's, we hung out on the back porches and roof tops, sunbathing, while my older sisters and teen cousins smoked cigarettes, of course some of those cigarettes smelled a little extra funky. I was told I could come up there to hang out, as long as I didn't tell anyone they were smoking. Meanwhile, my brother and my other goofy boy cousin would yell "Taxi!" at the cars below, and we would all laugh when the Taxi drivers would stop to look around for us. Sometimes, we were punks and even threw down water balloons!

Aunt Gigi was a clean freak, so she was probably inside cleaning while baking a German chocolate cake and eating ice chips. I swear her house always smelled of pine-sol and bleach! We had frequent trips to the brickyard mall for shopping and got our favorite chocolate covered pretzels. Once I pulled out my tooth inside the mall's bathroom with Aunt Gigi cheering me on, and in the morning I got a twenty dollar bill from the tooth fairy!! You better believe I saved my loose teeth to be pulled out by Aunt Gigi's after that!

We were always listening to Madonna on the way to get our VHS videos for Blockbuster nights. We ate pizza, drank RC pop, and ate Twizzlers while watching some scary movies like *Pet Cemetery*! Sometimes if my Aunt Gigi and Grandma Honey were too busy to watch us while my mom worked, we were sent away in the summers and winters for camp in Wisconsin or Michigan, where we would make S'mores by fires and go horseback riding. One year my siblings and I all went up to winter camp in Michigan, and we had to change our clothes frequently, not from the snow, but from peeing ourselves from laughing so hard going down the toboggan runs. We might have "accidentally" knocked down this very spoiled snobby girl in a bright pink snowsuit that everyone nicknamed Pinky. I know kids can be kids!

The counselors saw how she was so mean, yet they decided to show her "love" by hosting a girl's night makeover for her in the cabin. She was so happy; she twirled around with joy while the rest of us rolled our eyes, but it was a good thing for her. Then when summer came, my mom decided to split us up and had me go alone this time, so that meant no siblings for back up. I agreed only if she would buy me the Natalie Imbruglia cassette. So she did and I hopped on that bus listening to "Torn" the entire ride there. I went away solo to this ritzy acting camp where I met so many boys and girls. I made so many friends, yet I wanted to go home because my head kept itching. My mom wouldn't believe that I caught lice at such a prestigious camp.

Billy Zane went there from the *Titanic*, a very infamous movie at that time, so there's no way lice would find us, right?! Possible transmission culprits included sharing bunk beds in small dorm rooms and exchanging all the wigs while performing. I really had so much fun, though, and I always had the girls hang out in my room. I convinced this blue eyed boy that if he snuck into my dorm room I'd stay—and he did! We all ran around the dorms that night and into the fields, laughing wildly, free from the curfew and rules in place. I really had to go home, though, because of the lice, so my Mom and John picked me up. Thank God! Then about a year later that broken-hearted boy called me thinking about me: what a sweetheart! Going away to these camps was always fun and a welcome relief from our neglect and abuse.

Now, by our Grandma Honey's, we were allowed half a stick of gum, half of a pickle, and sometimes her Little Debbie oatmeal treats or even a piece of angel food cake, and of course more Blockbuster movies that consisted of the Wizard of OZ, Dirty Dancing, Willy Wonka and Ace Ventura. During the day, we played softball outside with the other kids in the cute little cul de sac she lived on for many years. Sometimes we got yelled at to go home, still full of sap from climbing and collecting pine cones from her neighbor's huge pine tree. My grandma always had her sports on local tv, like the Bulls: when they won their championships we would bang pots outside! If we were at Aunt Gigi's, we would set off fireworks wreaking havoc.

We literally spent our summers at the local pool all day long, and I mean all day long. The concession stand had these amazing gigantic chocolate chip cookies! I also just want to let you all know as a child, my siblings and I could've out-swam the entire US Navy Seals. We would call our mom "collect" on the payphones to come pick us up at the end of the night. We never wanted to go home, because, inside our house, we were scared by all the dysfunction. I definitely cried myself to sleep quite often because of the abuse I endured. I always felt unwanted; even as an adult I still struggle with those feelings. I really don't have a lot of great memories with my biological dad. He made me feel so unloved as a child and that made me question and hate my life.

My friend's mom always told me we chose our parents before we came here—and I would always say that I must have been pretty cocky to have picked out that guy! However, I do remember being sick one time and him holding the cup of apple juice for me so that I could drink out of it. I also remember some good times fishing. I remember him teaching me the "Our Father" prayer for my first Holy Communion (probably because he knew I would be praying it a lot having him as our father).

I definitely realized in my life, not one scar on my heart came from an enemy: they all came from people who "loved" me!

Sometimes when we were able to go to the other houses of his other children, my dad would often tell us they were the good kids, way better than us, and we were the "unwanted animals". For the most part, us kids all got along, but he would always try to divide us. Hearing him taunt us always hurt me inside, partly because they always did have a better life than us. My mom would have to take us to battered women shelter homes just to get away from him. We had to live all over the place in fear he would find us and kill us, as he threatened to do. We rented multiple homes in the same area every year just so we could go to the same school as our friends. We definitely ran out of gas in the car quite often. Sometimes we would have our water shut off or the electric, and we didn't even have a dining room table. That probably didn't matter much anyway because our fridge never had much in it! Our TV was on the living room floor and my mom slept on a dingy couch, so that we could all have our own bedrooms. One Christmas we came down the stairs and found absolutely nothing underneath the tree—just an apology note from our mom. (Don't worry ma; we forgive you!)

We also never got closure from our house; we had to leave it so abruptly. When my mom and I stopped by to gather some items, we saw the new renter was selling all of our belongings in a garage sale. All of my toys were in a bin for $5; I was so upset. Even our bunk beds were getting sold! My mom told me to step aside—not to listen to her arguing with the lady to stop selling our belongings to strangers. The wicked wrinkly mid-aged old lady didn't even seem bothered by me crying; she just kept on selling all of our stuff, guaranteeing we had to completely start all over!

I'll never forget the time my dad brought us to one of his other kid's birthday parties and knowing how much we loved to swim, he said to me and my brother and sisters, "put on your bathing suits; they have a pool." When we got there, we saw only a small mini pool that nobody could even fit in. He just laughed in our faces! Later, that family did end up getting a really nice big in-ground pool. He made sure to let us know what they had and what we didn't have. Then when we were leaving the party, one of the moms said "make sure you put their seatbelts on them and put the top down on the pickup truck." Most of the time we just rode in the back. She was so sweet; she treated us like she treated her own—with love and protection. He laughed and yelled back at her "don't worry, I'll just donate their bodies to science!"

Well, shortly after that, we got into a horrific car accident that he caused. There was a hit and run and my dad went to chase after the car that pushed another car into ours. During the chase we ended up slamming into another car and then right into a big tree in somebody's front yard. I kept screaming for him to pull over at the park to let us all out so we could just walk home safely but he continued on with his fat ego. He never listened! When the paramedics arrived I was so traumatized I even asked them to please slow down the ambulance as they raced my siblings and me to the hospital. I'll never forget I had my favorite bathing suit on that day and the emergency room doctors had to cut it off of me. I had such bad PTSD after that connected to driving cars. I still struggle with that. When we arrived home from the hospital, my dad said sorry to us kids and that from then on he would protect us, but I knew that he was full of it, because that knot inside my stomach just twisted and turned when he would talk.

My dad's abuse was so bad that he put my mom in the hospital once and he would even make fun of her while she recovered! I remember staying with my Aunt Gigi and anxiously waiting for my mom because I didn't understand what happened. My Aunt had me convinced my mom ate bad spaghetti left in the basement, but I wasn't buying it. I thought maybe it was her migraines she often suffered. I'll never forget asking that monster, "is mom in the hospital because she is sick in her head" (I didn't know how to talk about her migraines); I was young and naive. I just didn't quite understand at the time. He just laughed and laughed and said, "Yes, she is sick in her head alright." But in reality my mother basically suffered a nervous breakdown from all of the abuse she endured, so she had to be hospitalized. She completely shut down and didn't speak for a long time. She stopped talking for about a month. I couldn't even call her and I was so sad. I remember finally going to visit her; the sweet nurses gave my siblings and me Creamsicle ice creams as we all sat outside in a nice peaceful garden. My mother is so strong, stronger than you could ever imagine. She is a force to be reckoned with!

> *There is nothing stronger than a broken woman who has to rebuild herself right in front of the person who broke her down to the core! That woman I call my mother.*

The cops and DCFS got involved several times. He was so mean to my sister; he would call her names like "fat moose". He would hurt my brother by grabbing him by the throat and lifting him up against the wall. Sometimes Nana would just sit there and watch him and simply say, "you gotta do what you gotta do to have these kids listen to you." He would grab me by the back of my hair and lift me up and slap me in the face with his concrete hands. He even took me by the ponytail and cut it right off so I had to have a short haircut like a boy! My hair took years to grow back.

Once, I accidentally scratched his red pickup truck with my bike and he thought it was my brother, so he grabbed him by his neck and rammed his head right into the truck. In our driveway he killed an animal once and had a bucket of ammonia to clean up the blood. He told me to go over to the bucket and smell it. I thought it was water because it was clear, so I did smell it and I started choking and crying and he just laughed and laughed. He was also just so racist and said we could only marry Italians (insert eye roll here). We had a mailman of color and he would give him coffee but only in the same plastic cup every day and although it was washed, nobody else was allowed to use it. How insulting that was to such a kind human being and what a horrible message to teach us: to adopt hate and racism at such young ages. We then referred to him as Lucifer or Satan, and even the way he smoked his cigarettes was dramatic: the smoke would blow out of his nose just like out of the devil himself.

Sometimes my abusive dad would hit us with any object in sight, like a wooden 2x4, his belt, or an electrical cord from the vacuum. If he saw us with our elbows on the table while eating, he would stab us in the elbow with a fork! Once I had to go to school with blood on the back of my leg and my buttocks from him beating me with the vacuum cord. I guess before school that morning on the way to the bus stop I accidentally let our beloved dog Poochie out and she got hit by a car. I totally blocked that memory out. Thank God my sister told the principal about the beating so they were able to report that to the police and DCFS. When I arrived at school they called me down into the nurse's office and the nurse and principal asked me to take off my clothes to look at the marks on my body. The looks on their faces was one of such sadness... I kind of felt bad for them to witness my wounds. All the rumors about my siblings and me being "no good" died down that day. I returned to class, and my 5th grade teacher Mr. Z was about to cry; he hugged me so tight and told me if I needed anything I could just tell him. He was such a kind soul.

Throughout your life, I believe that sometimes all the pain and suffering, you're meant to go through that darkness, and in order to heal; you have to turn pain into light and help others. Turn your pain into meaning. Those people who took me on an emotional rollercoaster, misled me, confused me, and abused me: they were my first teachers for how to use my intuitive gifts. Being on a spiritual path does not prevent you from facing times of darkness. But it teaches you how to use the darkness as a tool to grow. Even the sun has to go through darkness to rise again each day. You, too, will rise again. Sometimes your path is more difficult, because your calling is higher.

"There's no coming to consciousness without pain."
– Carl Jung

If you or your loved ones are involved with domestic abuse situations, please seek help. Many resources exist to help you get out of an unhealthy situation. Start with the National Domestic Violence Hotline, 1–800–799–7233.

CHAPTER THREE:

Religion and Spirituality

> *"The soul given to each of us is moved by the*
> *same living spirit that moves the Universe."*
> *– Albert Einstein*

Thankfully, my siblings and I attended the Catholic Church and that really awakened my soul to the other side in many ways... My Mom would drive us to CCD class in this brown van; we jokingly called it the "shit box" because the muffler was so loud you could hear it from down the block. When she would turn the corner we would all yell, "Ma's home!" After our Saturday morning cartoons Mom would drop us off on those cold winter steps at the front of the church; that was probably her day of peace while we learned about saints and Angels. During mass the priest would always say we are all brothers and sisters, and to treat everyone as such. I thought to myself, "Oh great, all I need is more brothers and sisters!"

I had such a cool Catholic school teacher for CCD. She wasn't like the rest of the other teachers, who were stricter and colder. Mrs. C. was a short Italian lady who would talk loudly and passionately with her hands, and she always told us that swearing was okay as long as you didn't use God's name in vain or say Jesus Christ in a bad way. To be honest, for a Catholic school teacher, I thought she was pretty freaking cool; she would even talk about the angels and how they would try to show us they were around us and how they would give us signs they were near. She told us about how she helped this one lady with her groceries up the stairs to her apartment, and when she went to return to check on her the next day, she asked the neighbors where she was because she wasn't there. They told her nobody lives there. My teacher felt that an angel walked on Earth to offer a quick lesson of kindness. She would then tell us to be on the lookout for these angels in disguise. So I did. I took that message to heart!

I'll never forget the homeless man named Charlie to whom my siblings and I used to bring food and blankets. I always thought he was secretly Jesus, or an angel, in disguise. He lived at the end of our block in an abandoned horse trailer. In winter he would always say he was Charlie the Snowman, and in the summer, Charlie the No Man! I knew, because of my teacher, we were always doing the right thing by helping him.

Mrs. C had us all go around the class and talk about passed loved ones and how they would send us signs. My sweet friend in class talked about how she just lost her baby cousin in his sleep to SIDS; she and her aunts were baking cookies in the shape of angels for his funeral. When they went into his room, they found a white fluffy feather inside of his crib.

I always felt that it was different for Mrs C. as a Catholic teacher to talk about signs from the other side. I thought she was cool for being so spiritual. Mrs. C. wasn't like the others and I felt having her in my path really opened me up to my abilities. So when I would go home I would always wonder what being inside heaven would be like. I started writing letters to God and in first grade I even wrote a book about Angels coming to me at night. I started finding solace with the Angels, and when I started to see Spirit, I often felt comforted. I never met her, but I would see my mom's grandma in my bedroom at night; I knew it was her from a picture on my Grandma Honey's night stand. Sometimes, a man was with her, as well; I felt he was her son, one of my mom's favorite uncles, who passed away. He was an amazing artist and painter, and my mom put one of his paintings of a pink ballerina dancer in my bedroom. I think he was just trying to make his spirit known. I would also see souls I did not recognize, and that would frighten me because I knew how they died and sometimes those deaths were self-inflicted. Apparently, a previous owner of one of our houses committed suicide by hanging himself in one of the bedroom closets. That's when I started to fear death and dying.

As you can imagine, I would be up most of the night, and when I would cry for someone I was often dismissed and told to go back to bed. During the day at school, I would be so exhausted.

(*I have to add that if your children experience spirits in their rooms, try telling those spirits to leave and set boundaries. You can also get instructions on clearing their space with white sage. If those spirits are significant loved ones, just tell them goodnight*).

I was still so young so I didn't really know anyone who had died, except for my older sister's friend. This one boy we used to go to the pool with every summer; he and his best friend would show up, always so full of energy; we had so much fun together. They would do back flips off the diving boards along with my goofy brother, Antonio. That boy got into a fight with his mom one day so he was grounded from the school dance; he was so upset he unfortunately committed suicide. Shortly after his passing, his mom came to our house. She was sitting down at our kitchen table weeping while talking to my mom and dad. I was listening by the doorway, trying to keep my distance, so they didn't see me listening. I remember hearing his spirit say to me, "Tell my mom I didn't mean to do it; I thought she would find me in time. I'm so sorry."

I didn't know where this spirit was coming from, but at the same time, I felt natural somehow, hearing from Spirit, having his soul talk to me, without fully knowing that's what was happening. I didn't understand my abilities at that time. My heart ached for the boy's mother, but I was too nervous to tell her that message so I held it in. Now I know she was led to our house to receive the message I held in—and also to send a message to my dad about loving your kids right. It felt odd to me, watching her sit there talking to my abusive father about this, especially to one who takes his kids for granted so much: a true Dr. Jekyll and Mr. Hyde!

After they were done talking, I was in the bathroom with my mom and my sister talking about why dad (I use that term loosely) even cared to comfort the grieving woman, and of course he was listening and dragged me out right by my hair. You can bet I kept writing letters to God and the angels. I don't know why, but I would put them on the kitchen table, in the same way children put cookies out the night before Christmas and Santa is coming. So, of course, my dad would read them as if he was God, but that's ok. Somehow, whatever I asked for in those letters, God did deliver.

Shortly after the incident with the grieving mother and my school calling DCFS, my prayers were answered: DCFS took us away from our dad. We were so thankful to live with our grandma right after that. A part of me would of course remain fearful of my dad and afraid he would find us and hurt us again. But then there was also this part of me that felt like I needed to forgive him and make sure he wasn't lonely once we were all out of that house away from him. I even made him a small dinner of chicken drumsticks and a side dish, and I rode my bike to leave it by the side of the door with a note. I guess I felt he never really had the love he was supposed to get from the beginning of his life from his parents.

> *"Be the Love you never received."*
> *– Rune Cazui*

At a young age, I felt the angels always guided me to do the right thing even when that was hard to do. I always chose forgiveness and empathy. I always wanted to display the love I never received. I wish my dad had done the same thing, but maybe that was a part of our pact before we got here!(I made quite a few pacts in this book) In my Soul Group, he was to play the "bad guy" in my life, so that I could take this trauma, heal from it, and help others with my story, just like I am doing now. I was hurt and angry about my childhood and what bled into my adulthood. I could have found ways to take my suffering out on him, but I chose forgiveness, instead. Forgiveness is so important. However, forgiveness doesn't require reconnection!

Spirit wants us to know, in regards to this story, when life gets hard, remember, much beauty remains left to see, many adventures await to be had, and more love exists than you ever thought possible, if you just hang on.

Maybe I can't stop the downpour,
but I will join you for a walk in the rain.
– Anonymous

CHAPTER FOUR:

Premonitions of the Empath

As I continued to grow and mature, I felt that my abilities grew stronger. I started having life altering premonitions that would come true—and gut feelings around certain people. I would have dreams about people being pregnant before they even knew! I would just sense someone I knew was pregnant. For most of my life, I was always trying to make people around me laugh, and, yes, I was even named class clown one year. I think I found humor as the cure to the pain I had, as well as for being an empath, thus for the pain I absorbed from people surrounding me, especially at school.

One October night when I was in the sixth grade, we had a sleepover at my best friend Vanessa's house. I grew close to her family and her sweet father, because he was so nice to me, and he had such a gentle soul, unlike my dad. He was always laughing at me and saying in Spanish, "Ay, Abril," which means, OH April. We were getting ready to go to a haunted house. He was standing by the fence, waving goodbye as we got into the car. Vanessa yelled out, "Bye, Daddy, I love you," and I said, "Bye, Daddy, I love you, too."

We laughed, but then I got this really bad feeling in my gut. For some reason I felt really sad saying goodbye to my friend's sweet dad. We went to the haunted house, had so much fun, and came back, went to sleep, but were awoken in the middle of the night by the police at the apartment door. Vanessa's father had tragically passed away in a single car accident on the highway that night. I'll never forget the screams Vanessa's mother let out, screams which shook me to my core. She just kept screaming;

we were so scared. We jumped out of bed to see what was wrong, my heart was racing. We were then brought upstairs to her aunt's apartment, so she could watch us, because Vanessa's poor mother had to go identify her husband's body. It was still the middle of the night, so I didn't call my mom to go home.

Vanessa's family lit prayer candles; we tried so hard to fall asleep, but we just couldn't. I was staring at the flame on the candle; I felt so sad. I felt so responsible for knowing beforehand something wasn't right. I felt cursed. I developed anxiety. I kept trying to comfort Vanessa and remind her of our last goodbyes with her father and how we said "I love you" last.

When I returned home that morning, I was so shaken up, I had my mom stay in the bathroom while I took a bath because I didn't want to be alone. You see, being psychic isn't always what gets portrayed on tv. In the 90's, at that time, the only psychics we saw in the media were John Edwards, Sylvia Browne, and Miss Cleo. People thought psychic sensibilities were woo woo voodoo type stuff. If I went to doctors, they would just say I was an anxious child. I didn't need a medical solution; I needed a spiritual one! Nobody around at that time was available to help me with my abilities. I also never really told my mom about what I was experiencing; I was so little I didn't understand my abilities.

During the day while in elementary school, I would know things about people around me, like that my teacher was suffering from depression and alcoholism; then sure enough, we would learn he took a leave of absence for about a month.

We also had a very sweet lunch lady, Mrs.Ollie, with big teased-out black hair (big hair was in back in the 80's/90's). We could tell she just loved her job being with all of the children. Mrs. Ollie never missed a day! She had such an angelic spirit about her. One day she wasn't around anymore and I felt this overwhelming feeling of sadness: a sensation that she wasn't alive anymore. She was suffering from cancer and the other lunch ladies and staff didn't want the rest of the children to know that she was sick and then passed away. I knew it, though. I felt her soul around us. I felt the emptiness in the room from the other lunch ladies. I felt their pain and the grieving look in their eyes. So I finally asked Mrs. Julani, another sweet lunch lady, where Mrs. Ollie was. Mrs. Julani said she wasn't here, but tried not to go further into any details…until I said to her, "she died, didn't she?" Mrs. Julani choked up with tears in her eyes and asked how I knew? I said I felt her soul here with us and it just made me so physically sad that I had to ask her whereabouts. I felt her soul wanted the staff to talk about her memories with the children and that she was peacefully in Heaven now. Mrs. Julani seemed relieved in some ways to finally be able to talk about our beloved Mrs. Ollie.

Sometimes, I would look at classmates and just know what their worries were. I would feel so bad for them if they lost a loved one. I was very empathic, so I would take on feelings from people as if they were my own. Since I was little, I was constantly seeing faces at night and people standing in my room. Then, like multiples, one after another, more spirits appeared. I'd tightly close my eyes, but Spirit continued to show me another person, one after another. I didn't recognize these people, but I knew they were here from all over the world, yet they were from Heaven. I felt they were lining up to let me know my time had arrived to be of service to those here on Earth and in Heaven, but I just wasn't ready for all of this. I didn't understand "why me!"

"The intuitive mind is a sacred gift and the rational mind is a faithful servant. We have created a society that honors the servant and has forgotten the gift."
– Albert Einstein

My mom would take me to the doctor because I was completely fatigued and drained. Even my Lab results always came out normal and my iron levels were never off; I went to therapy but nothing ever really helped because my struggle was spiritual. Remember, we are all spiritual beings having a human experience! As I continued to get older, my abilities grew and grew. I gravitated to my beautiful teacher in 8th grade; she had curly hair like my mom and was very soft spoken as well. One day she announced she was pregnant with her first baby, and I was so happy and excited for her because I just loved babies. I had a dream that she had the baby early and that the child was really dark because sometimes when babies aren't fully developed they appear darker. While in class I felt a little funny around her the next few weeks at school, since I had that secret. She didn't show up one day, and I was concerned. Then I got sick, and when I returned to school, as I will never forget, this kid that sat next to me said Mrs. L was in school yesterday and had pictures of her baby: she ended up delivering early and the baby passed away peacefully in her arms. He said he was shocked because the baby was so dark! I felt shocked as to how I dreamt this and then it happened.

I told my best friend Savana about my dream, and she confessed to me how she would have feelings and dreams and premonitions as well, so I finally had someone to talk to about my gifts. Savana once had a visit from her beloved Aunt in a dream; in that dream her Aunt told Savana she's the only one who could see her—also to wish her other Aunt a happy birthday. When she called her mom to tell her about her dream, her aunt was actually there with her mom, and so she was able to wish a loving Happy Birthday to her from Heaven. Savana's Aunt then continued to come to her in dreams to warn her, as well, about actions that needed to be taken care of immediately, often concerning one of her young sons she left behind. Savana did so, and, without knowing, she became a vessel from the other side just like me. Savana and I lived right across the street from each other, and we had an instant connection. We would literally say how we were soul sisters because we were psychic and had strong ESP sensations connected to each other. We would think of one another and then the phone would ring. We could sometimes just look at each other and know things without even saying a word. We weren't just goofy teenagers with mood rings, I swear, because we still talk to each other almost every day and we are in our mid 30's!

When I got into high school, some of my friends knew about my abilities. But we still would just laugh about them, until one time I dreamt about my friend Camila and her brother, who was heavily into drugs at the time. In my dream he was in a coffin dead. So I called her up the next morning and told her about my dream and she was so worried because he was missing all weekend! I told her not to worry. I felt that maybe my vision was a sign of how badly he needed help before he ended up dead from all of the partying and drugs he was doing. She agreed and told her parents the concerns about her brother, and they found him, and her parents put him in a very expensive rehab treatment center. I have to say he is fully recovered up to this day and such a loving amazing guy.

Sometimes I would have recurring dreams about being on airplanes and see them crash into shiny windows of a building, and then my junior year of high school 9-11 happened. I was so confused as to how and why I sensed this horrific tragedy.

That was a very hard time for me—to see every single news station with the 9-11 aftermath—so I found one single channel that had actual shows to watch, alone in my bedroom in disbelief. I would dream about natural disasters as well, like tornadoes; I would also see so much water flooding in and then the tsunami hit the Indian Ocean in December 2004. Sometimes, I would get these premonitions and never really know when they would occur or where. You would think, trying to navigate through high school was hard enough on a hormonal teenage girl, so let's just throw some strong psychic medium abilities on top of that as well!

I had this one teacher who had beautiful crystal blue eyes, and she was around the same age as my mother, so of course, once again, I felt a connection to her. She was my Biology teacher, and I was a talker; I always had to stay after class and help her grade papers, so some of my friends C's turned into B's. (Yes, Camila and Savana, you can thank me for that.)

One time I was feeding the biology department's crayfish, and the lid fell off of the food and the entire bottle of fish flakes fell into the tank. I tried to scoop out as many as I could, but I abandoned my effort and, unfortunately, the crayfish overate and died, so I went from grading papers to staying after school to cleaning fish tanks for a week. The teacher was upset with me, but she had a couple boys of her own, so she just thought my punishment was sufficient enough. She took a leave of absence for a while when her husband suddenly passed away. When she finally came back, she cried to the classroom, telling us what happened. That's when I started to sense Spirit more and more. She came to school full-time and pushed through her grief as all of us students tried so hard to be good to her. Unfortunately, one student was not sympathetic. My teacher had to make the announcement to the class, crying tearfully, that someone had stolen her laptop, and that's where she kept all her grades for all of her students, and she desperately needed it back. She said, "I know my husband is up there watching over me, and I know he will help find it or find out who took my computer." I sat there with so much sadness listening to her that day, and I did feel her husband around us.

Shortly after her class I had lunch period; while I was waiting in line with such a broken heart for my teacher's situation, this boy walked up to me. He said, "hey, look what I got in my backpack, Mrs. B's computer. I took it." He was so happy about it. I felt he was led right to me. I said to him, "you've got to give it back; she was crying, and she needs it back, and she's going through a really hard time because of the terrible recent loss of her husband." I knew in that moment that her husband had me help this idiot get in line. So I went to the Dean's office, and I said, "listen, I know who stole Mrs.B's laptop, but if I tell you, you have to promise me that you won't expel him; he's just an idiot." The Dean agreed he wouldn't expel him, but he would still get in trouble for it, which he did, and had two weeks of suspension. I then went to Mrs. B's room, pulled her outside so nobody would see us talking, and I told her, "I know who stole your laptop. He's going to give it back, but don't tell anybody I told you." She didn't tell anyone, and she got her laptop back. A sense of relief came over her and me at the same time. I know her beloved husband was helping her by working through me that day. I'll say this as many times as I can: I seem to have this light above my head that the other side can see so that I serve as a way to send messages to their loved ones or help in any other way I can.

*"We are each of us angels with only one wing
and we can only fly by embracing one another."
– Luciano de Crescenzo*

CHAPTER FIVE:

My Mother's Knight in Shining Armor!

As I continued to grow into a young adult, by this time, my mom and my step dad, John were well established; they pretty much started dating when I was in elementary school, and I felt having my step dad in my life helped heal parts of myself much damaged. I felt so safe when I was with him, especially when riding in cars. He was absolutely nothing like my first dad! He was a very well respected police officer of the community. When it was my time to start driving, he taught me how to drive, not my mom. John took me to get my drivers license, and when we rolled up in his luxurious Audi, he told me, for a good laugh, to tell the driving instructor that this car was my Sweet 16 birthday present.

One time, he even taught me how to drive a stick shift in his then two seater Audi TT in a Kmart parking lot. Yes, he had a love for luxurious cars! Naturally, I wanted to take his car out onto the streets: I had already scared all the geese in the parking lot and thought why not scare the rest of the community as well! We approached this hilly road where the trains crossed. On that same road back in the day we would often scream to our mom to drive faster in our shit box to make us fly over the tracks so we could all laugh and say "wheeeee!" (Maybe that's why the muffler was broken and loud!) All of a sudden I could hear the train's horn blaring. A train was coming up ahead, and not knowing if I would make it, I shifted gears and whipped that bad boy up and over the train tracks. We flew up into the sky like in that scene from E.T. and once we high fived Jesus and Mother Mary I stopped the car on a less busy street and got out. He took over: stick shift was just not right for me. Nope, I would stick to automatic! I swear we both crapped our pants that day and never spoke of it again. I'll certainly never forget the look he gave me when we switched driver seats!

"There's a lady who's sure all that glitters is gold, And she's buying a stairway to Heaven."
– Led Zeppelin

I could close my eyes now without worries: I finally had a male figure in my life who stepped up like a father should. When I started dating. he would often give me his opinion on the guys, or he would just run their license plates to see if they had any outstanding warrants! We grew close, and we hung out often for weekly dinners with some deep conversations. We even went to many Cubs games together. My step dad John showed up big for me and my siblings, during graduations and birthdays, and even for inevitable heart breaks. Whenever I would mess up, he was right there to comfort and correct me.

Thanks to John, I was also able to watch my mother heal and feel safe. My step dad would write her love letters and sometimes leave her parking tickets on her car that just said "I love you" on them. My mom now had cards for anniversaries and Sweetest day and Valentine's Day. I also collected my share of birthday cards and graduation cards from my step dad. He was just so loving and thoughtful. I wanted to be like him and help others, but I didn't want to have to carry around a gun! He encouraged me to become a nurse, and so, I did, but not right away. It seems I had a few more lessons to learn.

"You can't go back and change the beginning, but you can start where you are and change the ending." -
– CS Lewis

CHAPTER SIX:

Soul Groups and Life Lessons

I was waitressing at the time and continued to have nursing school in the back of my mind, but I was having so much fun working with my high school friends at a local sports bar. Still, I kept having nudges from the other side, though I foolishly ignored them. I continued to have dreams about passed loved ones. I would sense things around people, but I sort of just got used to that and figured Heaven allowed for these insights. I was busy trying to be just a typical twenty year old dancing away on the bar tops! I unintentionally avoided deeper thought about my mediumship.

I had this manager who was really nice and fun, but then strangely mean, even cruel, when he was drinking. One night, I had this different group of people come in to eat; I could tell they were not from our country. Everyone working with us just kept staring at them. They were people of color and had a different appearance about them. They had bigger stomachs and barely touched their pasta! They even put ketchup on their pasta; I thought to myself, who does that? My manager was so drunk and just kept making fun of them and calling them names. When it was time to pay their bill, they gave me a voucher that was all paid for, but it was for the pancake house next door. These people had accidentally walked into our restaurant, and my manager made it known he wasn't going to waive their meal for them. So, since I was waiting on them, I was pretty much stuck with the bill. One of the guys with them had on new shoes and new clothes, clearly beyond his means. My manager just kept making fun of them and telling me I wasn't going to make any tip off of that table. He was trying to get me upset, but I made the decision to choose compassion and to help them. One of the males in their group stood up and didn't speak any English. He tried to sneak out and leave, and, when I saw him, he tried to trade me his watch to help pay for the meal. He looked frightened. They were probably so scared, not knowing what would happen to them. In their minds, they could be hurt or killed for their meal. I felt bad and declined the offer of the watch. I went into the payment portal and discounted their meal; I just paid for all of it. Eventually, a man who helps the group came down from their local hotel to explain that they were a group of refugees from Africa; they came here with absolutely nothing but to seek asylum. Everything they had with them was given to them through his charity work. He apologized for not steering them in the right direction. He was so exhausted from all of the traveling that he went to lay down for a bit. As I held back the lump in my throat, I told him, that's ok, they can leave now, they were all taken care of.

We all Bleed Red.

What a dose of reality I was given that night. I remember running straight into the bathroom and calling my mom, crying, because that was the moment I found out what a refugee was. I felt so bad. They were so afraid and beaten down; I never wanted anyone to be afraid of me. They still had so much fear in their eyes from their trauma back in their homeland; their distended stomachs were from being so malnourished. I still feel so sad, as if I could have done more for them. I remember wrapping up all of their food in hopes they would enjoy their pasta later. I cried so much that night: God decided to raise my awareness with those refugees. A few years later, I found out that the manager died from heart-related issues. He then came to me in a dream and said that, in that moment, he was part of the plan. He was testing me like God wanted him to do so, and that I did indeed pass. I remember waking up, saying to myself, I knew it! I knew that he was yet another "bad guy" teaching me a quick lesson from God.

> *People come into your life for a reason,*
> *a season, or a lifetime.*

Don't try to make people fit where they aren't intended, even a parent. We may all live in the same world, but we don't live in the same frequency. This misunderstanding of roles and frequencies causes us so much pain and brokenness. Try to find the lesson God sends you through those people to help build your own strength and character throughout your lifetime. I was sent many people for a reason, and you, too, are sent people to help mold you.

Even a drunken work manager or abusive father—even types such as these are brought to us to help build our characters and teach us lessons. God intends every single person you meet, and I truly believe that is part of "the plan" prior to coming here for Earth School. I've had people who taught me things that were bad, but I also had so many amazing teachers. My step dad John, my Aunt Gigi, and Grandma Honey are some of those blessed people.

Every person you meet, every single day, you meet for a reason—whether a homeless person on the street who needs something to eat, or someone who holds the door open for you when you walk through the Walgreens. I literally had amazing teachers throughout my school years. One was like the community father, he always had coffee or tea stains on his shirt, and he would threaten the class that he was going to pull out extra homework if we didn't listen, but of course he never would. He was the type that, if you had detentions, he would sign them off for you, just so you could go home. He would talk about his loving wife and praise his two children. He was a safe haven for so many kids throughout his teaching career. When I was over emotional and worried about the senior research paper, he saw that I was crying, and he genuinely took it easy on me so that I could pass and not have the trauma of being behind while everyone else graduated.

I had another teacher, a very beautiful Croatian woman. She was youthful, and when she was pregnant with her first child, she would talk about how much love existed between her and her husband. She would talk about how he would let her lay her head down in his lap while he gently plucked her eyebrows. Everyone in our class would just take in her beauty. I think that she was teaching all of us young girls how to love ourselves and how to be in a true loving relationship. She helped me once when I was going to prom my junior year with a senior boy. I didn't have a prom dress, so she gave me a beautiful pink bridesmaid dress she had. I was so grateful for her.

I am NOT a morning person, so I luckily had another teacher who would help me wake up in the morning, just to make it to school on time. She would call me every day, early in the morning. She was always so encouraging and would gift me things, like these gold bangle bracelets from the Mideast; her Muslim faith encouraged gifting people such items. She was so sweet and so proud of her culture and religion.

Some children go to school to learn, while others simply go to school to be loved!

You'll encounter people from all walks of life, so pay attention to all those people and all these "teachers"—teachers who walk alongside you throughout your lifetime. The good and the bad: they often test you to see how you're going to use your free will. At the same time, remember, a plan exists prior to you coming here. I know that although my first dad was very abusive, he was still very much a part of my Soul Group along with the others. He and I sacrificed our relationship in this lifetime, and even prior to that, so I could take that pain and suffering and turn it into love and light to help heal others.

"In the darkness there is always light. In the light there is always hope. In hope there is always love."
– Unknown

CHAPTER SEVEN:

Nurse April

"As a Nurse, we have the opportunity to heal the mind, soul, heart and body of our patients, their families, and ourselves. They may forget your name, but they will never forget how you made them feel." Maya Angelou

As time went on in my life, the other side was always trying to get me on the right path. I noticed I would go to estate sales and find lots of angels, angel candles and angel figurines, and, one time, at a garage sale, a book called *Ask Your Angels*. I was led down this path quite often, but I was just too lazy or too hesitant to understand these gifts. I finally decided to enroll into nursing school, at the time, I felt that was my true calling. I definitely read interesting books while in school, all medical, of course, so nothing to explain the spiritual things I was to encounter as a nurse.

As a nurse, I had these patients Phil and Joe, both in hospice in the same rooms together. Phil was an old school Italian man who would come to the nursing home to visit his wife every single day. She had severe dementia and would barely talk, but he would come to make sure he spoon fed her meals. It was so beautiful to witness the way he took care of her. He ended up with bladder cancer and then was admitted to the same floor as his wife so they could be with each other towards the end. To comfort him I found myself trying to spoon feed him the same way he did his wife, but he just kept declining the food. I felt hopeless but I believe he decided to go before his wife because he didn't want to be here without her—and of course to make sure Heaven was set up just right for his lovely wife.

His roommate Joe was elderly and non-verbal. He too was declining at a rapid rate, his organs shutting down. I kept having to check on him over and over. I noticed him raising his arms to the ceiling and staring above his bed as if someone were reaching towards him. I kept seeing sparkles around him. When I was putting cold wash cloths on him, I noticed he had tears in his eyes; he was in so much pain and suffering. I made sure he was getting frequent pain meds and other meds to drop his high fevers. Joe passed away surrounded by his only son and granddaughter. Afterwards, I was cleaning the room, and I found a beautiful plastic flower by his bed. I asked his family if it was part of his belongings and if the granddaughter wanted to take it, but she said no, the flower didn't belong to Joe. So I smiled and said, "Thank you, Joe": I just knew the flower was meant for me as a gift of gratitude.

Later that day I had to call Phil's son to get him back from out of town because his father didn't have much time. To witness death remains amazing and bittersweet! Phil waited for his son to get there to say goodbye, and then he passed away shortly after reuniting.

> *"A nurse is one who opens the eyes of a newborn and gently closes the eyes of a dying man. It is indeed a blessing to be first and last to witness the beginning and end of life."*
> *– Unknown*

I then had this sweet little Irish lady, Beverly, a teacher from Detroit, Michigan. She even had members of The Supremes as her students!

She would often say they were alright, but she didn't really care for their music because she was more into classical. I laughed because she was so nonchalant; I felt she didn't really soak in the fact that she taught really gifted students. Beverly had cancer and when asked if she would like to continue treatment she graciously declined.

She said she was wise enough and made peace with this life and was ready to go to the other side to join most of her loved ones. I remember her asking me to get her out of bed one last time so that she could stare out the window at the beautiful sunlight that reflected off the sheets of snow on that beautiful January day. She was only about 70lbs. I carried her like a baby and put her into her wheelchair while she just basked in the sunlight making her peace with God one last time. Even her cat named Bocelli joined her on her lap! I just sat there and watched her stare out the window. She sat quietly and ran her fingers through her silver hair while closing her eyes to feel the warm sunlight on her face. She absorbed all the life, energy, and warmth she could during her last days of life here on earth; it was so beautiful to witness. Then the souls started to fill the room to help her make her transition.

Once I put her back into her bed, she held on for a good two weeks while her only son came and stayed every day of the week. Only after her son whispered into her ear, "I love you Mom, but it's okay for you to go now," that his mom then made her transition to Heaven. I asked Beverly's son who Cecil was, and he said he was his dad. (although I knew it was the spirit of passed loved ones, I had to convince her son otherwise.) I told him his mom was reaching towards someone across the room saying the name

Cecil. He confirmed his dad had been gone for years. I knew his dad came to greet his mom to help her cross over to the other side. Right after Beverly's passing I saw sparkles and felt a little tingling sensation as if her soul was free and moving through me and all her loved ones present during the final moments of her passing. I had to take a moment to sit down because that feeling was overwhelming yet euphoric for me to experience.

> *"A nurse will always give us hope,*
> *an Angel with a stethoscope."*
> *– Carrie Latet*

Then there was Sterling. He was a patient that was a ward of the state. He would swear at me and tell me what the F*** was taking so long while I would give him his shots. He would try to get the aides to give him water and more ice chips even though he was on fluid restrictions due to kidney failure. But I loved him and I would check on him frequently; he was just so vulnerable, tiny, and frail despite having the mouth of a truck driver, but hey, that's okay, because I cursed like a nurse. So in our own twisted way we got along just fine. One day we had to send him to the hospital because he just got worse; I'll never forget seeing him sitting up on the gurney being wheeled out by the paramedics. We locked eyes and I just knew that he wasn't coming back. Days went by and he still didn't return.

One night I had a dream of him and he just stood there and said "thank you." The next day I went back to work and the hospital nurses kept calling for his next of kin, but wouldn't say because of HIPAA, and I said, he's a ward of the state and I can get you his social worker. She said thank you, because he's been passed away for a few days now and we need someone to come claim his body. I thought, wow, he came to me in the dream to say thank you!—probably because he was always so grumpy with me when I would try to take care of him. His appearance was so vivid; he just wanted to make sure to say thank you to his favorite nurse, and I thought that was so sweet of him.

My mom says that I became a nurse to understand the things that I do now with my mediumship. I couldn't agree more with my mama about that statement!

I had a Nurse friend from Russia named Natasha. I dreamt about her Baba (grandma in Russian). I dreamt her Baba was saying, "congratulations" and she was happy for her, and something about a gold necklace. So I told Natasha, who was spiritually open to my dream, and she was so happy, because she just finished nursing school and got her board exam results that stated she passed. Natasha had her grandma's gold necklace on for good luck during her test. She stated she never takes it off! I thought that was so beautiful: to relay such love to my friend; she was so close to her Baba and she never got the chance to say goodbye.

> *"The spiritual journey is the unlearning of fear and the acceptance of love."*
> *– Marianne Williamson*

CHAPTER EIGHT:

Aunt Gigi

I started to have more encounters in dreams with passed loved ones, but I shrugged many of them off, suspecting that's just how they come to visit us after they cross over. I then, unfortunately, lost my Aunt Gigi in a terrible car accident when I was in my 20's. Our family was completely devastated, and we did not understand why God took her away from us so suddenly. I now know her path and purpose was served. She came here to love and protect many children like myself, who never received the proper love and care at home. On the day of her wake I gently kissed her forehead in the coffin and told her thank you for saving us—for always being a safe haven to us and so many other children. She was beautifully laid to rest across from the kids' section in the cemetery.

After her passing I would help her daughter with her two-year- old and five-month-old boys because that's exactly what she needed at that time. My cousin actually had a premonition about her passing a few weeks prior to when it happened. I feel that dream was her Spirit Guide's way of getting her soul ready for her beloved mother's departure. She felt so lost, because her mother was everything to her, and those boys were everything to my aunt.

I knew I had to pick up some of the pieces to help my cousin during her deep stages of grief. I would care for her boys while she and her husband went back to work. I watched my cousin completely wither away. She, too, felt responsible for her sense of knowing tragedy prior to her mother's death, as if she could have prevented it. She was stick skinny and pretty much coasted through life, barely existing day after day. A part of her heart and soul died the day her mother died, never really to return.

I would always talk to my Aunt Gigi and ask her if I was doing things right for her boys, and I would pray for her. I again began to wonder what it was like inside Heaven and where she had gone after death. My cousin's two year old son would talk about seeing her at the end of his bed at night, and he would say, "Nani, I'm so tired; I don't want to play right now." He said she would sit there and poke at his feet, trying to get him to play.

One time I was sitting at the dining room table, and I could hear the children's toys going off in the basement, no one down there. Another time, I was feeding the boys at the table, and suddenly the TV shut off right in front of us. My cousin started to experience similar things as well, with the boy's toys going off at night when nobody was around. The doorbell would also start to go off and nobody was there. My cousin had a mobile CD player that played music and lights inside the crib for the baby. She put a Motown CD in there because it reminded her of her mom: that even started turning on out of nowhere. Oftentimes, my cousin sees beautiful cardinals almost every day in her yard, and she would acknowledge them by saying, "Hi, Mom."

Whenever I was on my way to see my cousin and the boys, I would look down in the street and find jewelry, but not just any type of jewelry: Catholic medals, pendants and crucifixes. I found a cross with little hearts on it and the blessed Mother Mary, and a Jesus pendant, and I knew these were signs I was doing the right things to help my cousin during her most difficult time of mourning. I know my Aunt Gigi was trying to get our attention. As the years would pass, she started coming to me in dreams and would say how she would be at the boys baseball games.

The boys are now teenagers, and one is very empathic and intuitive. When he was sleeping over at her house recently, he had a dream about a woman calling his name from the couch downstairs. She went to touch his arm, and when he woke up, he was standing in front of the couch! When she passed, he was only five months old so he doesn't really remember her, but I'm telling you, these grandchildren were her world. That shows you these bonds are everlasting. My cousin kept the family together after the passing of her mother by taking over the family traditions and having everyone over for the birthday celebrations and holidays at her house. She kept her brothers close to her and often took over a lot of what their mom did for them. I know that is exactly what my Aunt Gigi would have wanted.

Most recently, Madonna songs kept playing for me: I took that as a sign Aunt Gigi was around. That weekend my cousin's son was graduating high school, so I just thought those signs were once again my Aunt just sending her love. Before long we got a call that my cousin's husband had a major heart attack at work, and all he remembered was blacking out and hearing laughing from my Aunt Gigi! Doctors shocked him back so hard that he bit his tongue; he could hear those doctors saying, "Yes, we got a pulse; WE GOTTA PULSE! Welcome back big guy!" It just wasn't his time to go! Without a doubt, I know my Aunt Gigi was somehow involved in sending him back. Aunt Gigi is always around watching over and protecting everyone.

So one holiday season my Aunt Gigi came to me, so vividly in a dream and told me not to forget about my brother and to make sure he was at Christmas with us this year. She showed me the clam bowl used for holy water. I was so confused about this clam bowl. I told my cousin about that, and she said that when they were kids her mom had one of those clam holy water dipping bowls. My Aunt Gigi was religious, so that explains why I was finding all of the sacraments on my path as well. I kept telling the family I felt something was wrong with my brother, but they blamed my premonition on sibling rivalry. I didn't know what to do for him, but I kept getting repetitive gut feelings around him that something just wasn't right.

"Intuition is the whisper of the soul."
– Jiddu Kristnamurti

CHAPTER NINE:

Brother

Not until I was at work one day did I start to understand that dream, along with the serious concern regarding my brother Antonio. He called me crying and saying how he was reading the Bible and how many bad things will soon happen, just like they did in Haiti. He would talk about how when he was little he would have premonitions about Haiti and then many, many years later a massive earthquake hit there. My brother literally donated the rest of the money in his bank account to the Red Cross at that time because he said he felt responsible for knowing the earthquake was going to happen. He started to meditate and smoke a lot of pot and drink, thinking that would help take the edge off everything he was sensing and experiencing at that time, but instead that lowers one's vibrations, like leaving doors wide open in a bad neighborhood.

When I bought my first house I had Antonio move in with me so I could help him get on track. But I noticed he got worse, stopped eating and sleeping, and started to read the Bible and obsessively take notes. He started to do a lot of soul searching, asking questions no one really understood. His mental state got so bad that he would only eat canned foods and oranges because he thought he was being poisoned. Then he went to work one day and passed out and fell flat on his face and broke his nose. He became paranoid about the government and people tracking him on his phone. He would see and hear things that weren't there for others. He would meditate and tell me he would see visions of Jesus and that God told him that I'm the chosen one of the family. I now see what he meant by that. He finally came to me and my mom for help, so we took him to the hospital; they diagnosed him as bipolar schizophrenic. This diagnosis was a shock and devastating for us all; there's no cure, only treatment. I felt like I had completely lost my brother. I was mourning someone still here... He wasn't moving forward in life like he should have—and that broke my heart. He wanted a family and kids, but the severity of his illness made his dreams unlikely realities.

Antonio has been in and out of the hospital many times and we even hired lawyers to have the court mandate a monthly shot, because he refuses meds. He went on and off all of these different medications, and to be honest, I felt they made him worse. I also felt he too was gifted in many ways, but he was also so unhealed from our childhood trauma. That lack of healing got in the way of his life's full path and destiny.

I remember going to the hospital to visit Antonio. Michael, the psych ward social worker, allowed me to go beyond the family visiting room. I walked down that long hall not knowing why my brother wouldn't come out of his room. I stood in the doorway and there he was: swaddled in his bed sheet like a child staring out the window. He looked so lost and confused. I so badly wanted to help him snap out of it. This hospital was so old, too, and that floor reminded me of *One Flew Over the Cuckoo's Nest*. I felt there was no way people could repair themselves within the walls of a hospital room like that. I was so angry because our society is so backwards with the way we try to help and heal others.

My brother Antonio needed nature; he loved the outdoors. He was the type who did every major sport that belonged to every season. Whether Fall football, or snowboarding in the winter, or swimming throughout the summer, Antonio was involved! I approached him in that horrible room, "Antonio, it's me, April, your sister." He just screamed something so confusing; I'll never forget the words: "GET THOSE KIDS OUT OF THAT HOUSE!" I sensed he was reverting back to our childhood, as if his mind was racing backwards in time to things unhealed from our childhood.

Naturally, I became so hurt, angry, and scared to see Antonio like that. I turned around with tears rolling down my cheeks and walked down the hall back to where the social worker was, hoping he could console me with words of encouragement. I was so thankful he allowed me to try to get my brother to come out. He often needs meds to snap out of states like that. So I waited a week and went again on Sunday. While in my car I drove in silence listening to the tires roll on the crunchy cold pavement of that cold winter day. I turned on the radio and Adele's song "When We Were Young" came on, so I just absorbed the words into my soul. Those lyrics kept bringing me back to our childhood and how badly I wanted back those summer days and rooftop moments when we were just a bunch of free-spirited kids.

I started to cry and turned my car around; I thought to myself, "why go when he doesn't even know who I am, let alone what day it is!" I went back to visit him once his meds kicked in and we sat across each other laughing like a bunch of little kids again, with our mom in the middle of us coloring adult swear books I bought him (who doesn't love adult coloring books, let alone the swear word ones!). It was as if nothing had happened to him; he was brought back to us once again by his meds. For Antonio, when he is in a period of psychosis, he seems like an early onset dementia patient...and he doesn't recall any of it! His condition is harder on us than it is on him sometimes.

I know in my heart my deceased Aunt Gigi was trying to warn me about my brother to make sure he was included with the family. I know the other side can do this, and I know she saw what was going on with him and that he needed so much help at that time. I'd like to say Antonio is now healed and doing well, but he's completely not. He made his way out to California and went off his medications once again and now lives on the streets with his Bible in hand, telling people he is GOD. The sad thing is he was once so into health and fitness; he even created a gym in a bag that he got patented. His invention is just waiting to be promoted, but he took a detour. I truly believe his story is like that 90's song: "*What if God was one of us... just a stranger on the bus trying to make his way home.*" Antonio is just taking a different path, and I understand he might not fulfill his life's full path and purpose—or maybe he is exactly where he is supposed to be to teach others about the homeless and mental illness.

One of my favorite quotes is by Ram Dass: **"Treat everyone you meet like God in drag."** I feel such is Antonio's true message at this moment of time.

NAMI is a non-profit organization for the National Alliance of Mental Illness which helps those like my brother; I have donated to them in that area of California. I miss him so much. We've tried many times to get him help, but since he is not a harm to himself or others, the laws work against us as his family members. We constantly try to get him to come home, but he remains noncompliant.

I remember, as a child, I always had this recurring dream about Antonio and he was so lost and confused up on a cliff; I kept climbing up trying to save him. I believe that was a definite premonition. I'm hoping one day soon he will get the help he needs. He wasn't always like this, and sometimes the onset of mental illness comes on fast, like brain diseases such as Dementia and Alzheimers. Antonio was very popular and very well-liked by the girls. Even though I was a year older than him, some of my girlfriends dated him because he was so funny and handsome. One of my girlfriends even asked him to go to prom with her! He was always so fit and in shape; he probably could've been a sports model because he was so tall and handsome.

My brother Antonio was so funny, like Jim Carrey, and was constantly acting out those scenes from *Ace Ventura Pet Detective*. He was the one who did the senior year prank in high school: setting loose chickens in the hallways. What a riot to watch the security guards run after them! All in the school knew Antonio was the prankster guy, just like those on *Jackass*: probably where he got most of his ideas. One Easter, he even came down the stairs in one of my mom's floral dresses just to get a good laugh out of us all, and my mom was screaming, because he was stretching out her dress—but it was just so hilarious. He was constantly joking, because of course, that's how we kids dealt with the inner pain. One time he broke his arm at the skatepark, and when he called my mom to tell her she thought he was joking and hung up on him; she suspected he was always joking. Only when paramedics called her did she realize this broken arm wasn't a joke.

My poor brother, his illness can at times give us so much hope, like when he talks to us normally, but then by the next moment, he's not "all there", as if "the lights are on, but nobody's home."

"One love, one blood, One life, you got to do what you should. One life with each other Sisters, Brothers."
– U2

I truly believe our journey in this life together was all part of some plan. I believe my siblings and I got together in Heaven to make a pact concerning what burdens we were to carry for one another, just as long as we stuck by each other. Antonio was more like, "Hey April, on Earth, I'm gonna see, hear, and feel things that are not there, and convince people that I'm crazy, and you're gonna be challenged with hearing, seeing, and feeling things, too, that nobody else can experience, but you're the messenger. I am gonna let all of the world know the messages in my own way, too." What remains tricky for us is most people seek a medical solution to such behavior, when really what's needed is a metaphysical and spiritual solution to most madness.

All I ask is that you all send positive thoughts to Antonio; pray that he fulfills his purpose here in this life—that he serves the highest good of all concerned. The best place you can be is in someone else's thoughts and prayers!

Someday, more centers worldwide will exist for the mentally ill which touch base with the spiritual side, as well as the latest medical solutions. In the future, we should not see homeless people; they will be taken care of in the most respectful manner. That's what I hope for the future of my grandchildren's generation, if not sooner.

> *Hope itself is like a star—not to be seen*
> *in the sunshine of prosperity, and only to be discovered*
> *in the night of adversity.*
> *– Charles Spurgeon*

Call the NAMI Helpline at 800-950-NAMI, or, in a crisis, text "NAMI" to 741741.

CHAPTER TEN:

Sage Your Space!

When I bought my first home, weird things started happening, like light bulbs going out and fire alarms going off at 3 a.m.. Even when certain family members were over, my fire alarms would start going off as they walked past them. It was as if Spirit wanted that negative energy to leave. Once when my Nana and Aunts stopped by after years of me not seeing them, just so I could babysit my cousin's toddler while they went to a wedding, on their way out Spirit made its spirit known to get negative energy away. As they were leaving, right next to them, a fire alarm I had recently taken down started blaring, as if to tell them to "get the hell out"! Even a few days later my Aunt called me and we were talking about some very negative things my Dad did to people back in the day and, well, Spirit once again made the fire alarm above my head go off! So I stopped that conversation and hung up with my Aunt. I had outgrown these people and didn't need that negativity in my life or in my house. It was not a coincidence that these fire alarms kept going off!

I'd also see shadows and sparkles, and instantly, I felt a male spirit. I would get the chills. I would have dreams about not being able to breathe while grabbing my chest and reaching for the windows for help. I was outside one day, and one of my elderly neighbors, Ralph, came up to me. Ralph was a very talkative Italian man about 90 years old. He lived in the area for a very long time and knew it well. So I asked him who originally lived in my house. He told me how old man Jimmy died alone in his bedroom and how nobody knew, so he was found days later. Jimmy had a heart attack. I believe that's exactly what he was trying to show me in my dreams and that's why I experienced gasping for air, crawling to the windows for help. Ralph's wife Rosa was standing next to him; she started hitting his arm to tell him to shut up and not to scare me. I laughed and I said, "No it's okay, I already sensed Jimmy around!" That's when both Ralph and Rosa looked at me a little funny!

I went to a little shop far from my home that sold sage and crystals connected to psychics and mediums. I bought a book that, of course, I never read until much later, about getting to know one's spirit guides. I too often dismissed these spirits right in front of my face. I saw this lady waiting by the door for her client. She told me she was a psychic medium, so I told her what I was experiencing in my home. She told me to buy white sage and to sage my house clockwise in every dark space from top to bottom. I start at the front door and end at the front door. She suggested I tell the spirit to leave, because he displayed negative energy. I said I didn't feel he was negative, but she said since he's not respecting my boundaries and not allowing me to sleep, that his impact on me was negative. Once I set my boundaries and saged my space, I noticed right away the dreams stopped and everything I experienced during the day subsided as well between that spirit and me.

Not long after, Ralph passed away and his wife Rosa called me crying because she so desperately wanted a sign from her beloved husband. They had been married for over 50 years and it was hard for her to continue moving on without him physically here. So one day she called me up with a bit of confusion in her voice; she kept hearing knocking on her doors, and she thought maybe it was me. I laughed and said, "Rosa, how could it be me? I'm across the street inside my house. It was Ralph: you wanted a sign, so there it was." She said, "this is weird, I have to go," and hung up the phone on me! Sometimes, we just dismiss the other side when those spirits try desperately to give us the signs we asked for.

CHAPTER ELEVEN:

Motherhood

When I was pregnant I'd have to say Spirit honored me, letting me be peaceful and enjoy the moments of pregnancy as I was inviting these new souls into the world. I wasn't having as many dreams of passed loved ones or many premonitions. Spirit gave me my time to be still and bond with my baby growing inside. I felt such a deep connection to the other side; I glowed in a bubble of God's everlasting love. With both of my children, I knew every time I was pregnant and exactly what I was having. We, as women, invite children into this world, and that becomes a spiritual journey. We have mother's intuition: don't let anyone tell you differently. Women are portals from one world to the next. Women are very spiritual beings. I am almost convinced God is a woman!

I did have a dream of my obstetrician's father coming to me to tell her she was going to be okay. Of course, I never told my doctor this message because I didn't want to step into her energy like that. The majority of doctors don't believe in life after death. So I just keep certain messages to myself. It's funny though how Spirit always has a way of finding me as if I have a light over my head! Yep, I'm a lightworker! So when I was pregnant with my first child, I found out my favorite doctor was taking a medical leave of absence and possibly retiring due to hearing loss related to a virus. She could no longer work in the field and deliver anymore babies. I felt sad because she started the practice and was damn good at it, too. When I was pregnant with my second child about two and a half years later, I found out her hearing came back and she was doing better with cochlear implants. How comforting her dad came to me to let me know she would be okay!

Yes, I did have the mother's intuition "on steroids" and would know when my kids would get sick or something was about to happen. I kept calling the school to have the bus stop changed, because I just felt something was off. We had all of these cars and semi-trucks flying down our street, because we live in a busy industrial area. I had a dream about my son getting hit by a car, and then, within weeks, a lady went through the bus stop sign and almost rolled over him.

"The power of intuitive understanding will protect you from harm until the end of your days."
– Lao Tzu

Another time, I kept telling my son's pediatrician something was off about him. I felt that he was having seizures shortly after receiving his vaccines, but the doctor kept brushing me off and said no, I'll refer him to a neurologist. The doctor still gave him his vaccines that day, and literally, when we left the office, my son started having seizures in his car seat. We went straight to the hospital where he stayed the week for heavy testing. Everything came back normal; he hasn't had a seizure since that day, and he hasn't received vaccines since then, either.

Moms, all I have to say is, your children are a part of your heart and soul, and if you feel some realization in your gut, that feeling is genuine intuition and your guardian angels. Our children are the only ones that hear our heartbeat from the inside; so trust that strong, loving connection!

Times will come when you take your kids to doctors and you just feel something is off. You have to go with that gut feeling. My son, of course, like many kids, stuck something up his nose and got it stuck deep, and infection set in. I took him to an ENT who didn't even have the patience for his crying and wanted to put him under anesthesia just to get out the pieces of wipes he stuffed up there. I cried and set up the surgery date, but after checking in with my intuition at the last minute, I cancelled and found an ENT who was a mother of two. She listened to me over the phone, and when we went to our appointment, she was able to get the piece of wipes out within minutes. No anesthesia was needed! We used this cool papoose swaddle thing, and yes, he kicked and screamed, but it worked. I'm sure that other doctor was so pissed, but I don't care. I felt better knowing my son was awake for his procedure. Of course, his mishap will go down "in the books", and I will bring it up at his wedding many years from now.

Gut feelings are your guardian Angels!

While out running errands, I was on my way to the bank, and our favorite bank teller, who gives my kids lollipops, had a grandma pass away; I would feel her grandma push through to send her a message. I would hold back and start to feel so anxious, and I would have to turn my car around and go home. I basically didn't even feel comfortable driving or going to public places anymore, especially if I had my kids with me, because I didn't fully know how to set boundaries with the other side just yet.

Sometimes if I was with my kid's at a birthday party, some random gramma would walk up to me and talk to me about her deceased son, and then the name Mikey would pop into my head and I would ask her what his name was, and yep, Mikey it was! His spirit would then show me how he died, as gramma was telling the story, but he would fill in the other details as she went on. I would hear how his fall came from his drinking too much and how his daughters don't come around because he was given a bad name by his ex wife. Gramma would tell me how she misses his kids, and I felt compelled to tell her that they're in pain, missing dad, so not to hesitate to reach out. I think I did a good job encouraging her to do so, yet Spirit was the one giving the nudge. I felt good sharing these messages, but at the same time, I felt a huge responsibility for fully healing the families, and that made me anxious.

I feel like sometimes motherhood awakens us all. Remember my best friend Camila from high school: she was pregnant with her first child and under a lot of stress at work, plus our very close childhood friend passed away from a drug overdose a few years prior. That deceased friend decided to come to me in a dream, and he kept trying to get Camila a car seat in her favorite color teal. He had a sense of urgency in the dream, as if he were trying to warn her. I told Camila about my dream and to make sure she had a car seat properly installed. Our spirit friend was definitely trying to get our attention: Camila ended up having her baby prematurely and needed her car seat earlier than expected. Camila even told her brother about my dream, because he was so close to our dear friend; as soon as she told him, he got the chills. He, too, recently had a dream about our childhood friend. My experience provided the confirmation he needed to know our friend was still watching over us, guiding us from inside of Heaven.

Remember, be open. Be willing to talk about what the inside of Heaven is like, and you, too, will be able to "see" the amazing things that happen. Don't hesitate to go INSIDE YOUR HEAVEN!

Camila completely awakened spiritually after that, and when she most recently had her second baby, she called to tell me about her dreams now and how her deceased co-worker came to her in a dream; his spirit reminded her of a fun loving teacher we shared in high school. In the dream, he said to her that in order to get to Heaven, in life we have to go through the "haunted house" first. We both laughed about that, but I think the notion is so true. I'm writing this book in the middle of 2020. (*Google this year, and you'll completely understand!*)

You're probably wondering if my son and daughter share my abilities. I believe both of my beautiful children do. My son Stephen is very much an empath. Since he was a toddler, he would have dreams about ladybugs, and he would wake up so happy. He kept telling me about these ladybugs, and we would find ladybugs in our bedroom even in the middle of winter. My children never met their paternal grandfather; he passed from cancer before they were born. It wasn't until I found a Thank You card from him with tons of ladybugs all over his card, did I realize how he was trying to communicate to his grandchildren and provide love from the other side. Stephen as well will often talk about the premonitions he has within his dreams that come true the following day or so.

Both of my kids have talked about shadows in their room. My daughter is very clairvoyant and clairaudient, meaning she sees and hears Spirit. She will talk about spirits as if they're right next to her, and they sure are! There is no veil for children, so, often-times, your baby will be smiling or playing, and there is nobody in the room. I encourage you to always keep an open mind with your children, because they're so open to the Spirit world, and we could learn so much from them.

"Children are not things to be molded,
but are people to be unfolded."
– Jess Lair

CHAPTER TWELVE:

Miscellaneous Downloads

As the years went by, I became more aware of just how much Spirit was like birds on the cable lines, like a city of angels, looking down on us willing to spread messages. I once followed this missing child case on the news the next couple towns over. The boy missing was wearing these pajamas with the Disney Pixar movie *Cars* on them; he was about the same age as my son at the time. My heart ached to see he was just such a precious soul with so much left to give. His mom came on the news pleading for her son to come back, saying he was taken by people who pulled off in a van. I, however, saw right through her lies. I reached out to a friend, a police officer working that case. I said, "she's lying right through her teeth, something doesn't sit right." I sensed she had total involvement in her son's disappearance.

He said he couldn't talk about the case at that moment, but they knew. I went to bed that night; I dreamt of the boy's body in the river close to our area. I woke up in the middle of the night—such a huge download! I was so shaken up by this little boy's story, and I just cried. I messaged my friend and asked him where they looked for him. He said a key announcement would be publicized later that day. I wanted to know if they looked down by the river, but I was too afraid to say anything. Later that day, the evening news reported the mother and her boyfriend killed the boy and dropped his body in the river near our area. I was completely shocked as to how I knew this detailed information and as to who gave it to me in my dream. I'm certain the angels can see everything; as well as who we are connected to.

I no longer watch the news: that wasn't the last time I became attuned with homicidal incidents in the area. Even when the news broadcasted the Boston marathon, I remember the scene looked eerie and gray to me. Something didn't feel right about that day, and it almost didn't feel real. Later that day, they reported the bombing, and then the manhunt began.

One time this police officer called in shots fired, and another manhunt began, but then, again, I knew the story was off and that the officer's wound was self-inflicted for insurance purposes. I reached out to a friend I grew up with to get his input; he is a forensic ballistic scientist. I told him what I felt, but once again, I was led by Spirit to someone actually working on this case who couldn't disclose any information. For days, his family and the media portrayed the suspect officer as this hero and as a man in uniform who serves and protects the public with integrity and grace. Turns out this police officer and his wife and son were involved in stealing money from fundraisers for children, to the tune of $100k! He was on duty when he committed suicide to try and get money for his family from life insurance; people were starting to find out about the missing money, and he wanted to make his shooting look like someone else did it, so his family would get more money since he was on duty.

I noticed that while I was around certain family members, I could feel what they were going through before they would bring it up, or I would dream about their troubles. I was still close to my cousin on my dad's side, although he lived out of state. We would frequently talk and put each other in check about unhealed things from our childhood. He came to town for my Nana's memorial when she passed away and I felt that knot in my stomach again when he was about to leave as if that was going to be the last time I saw him. We often talked about the mother of his twin boys and I felt that something was off and I kept telling him she was cheating on him, but he wasn't convinced. Within weeks of him returning home he fought with her and her guy "friend", who shot and killed my cousin. I once again felt so helpless trying to warn him. He left behind three kids, twin boys and a girl.

CHAPTER THIRTEEN:

Loss of My Safe Haven

The anxiety continued, and that's when I kept telling my mom that I had felt there was something wrong or off about my step-dad John. She, of course, dismissed me like, no he's all good, but I would get so anxious, and I would wake up in the middle of the night. I just felt so unsettled, but I couldn't put my finger on what it was.

We were at my sister's baby shower, and I just felt a shift of energy around John. My step dad was a very private person, but something like this I would have expected him to tell me. Maybe he was scared and he didn't want to talk about his health troubles: he just wanted it gone… I found out about my step dad's cancer when my sister mentioned my mom couldn't be with her when she might deliver her first son because she needed to be at John's surgery. That's when she told me John has cancer. My heart dropped; I picked up the phone and called my mom, and I was like, John has cancer! She was at work; I insisted she tell me at that instant. I felt like I was going crazy, like when I noticed my brother Antonio's signs and symptoms of mental illness nobody believed me and now sensing everything painful surrounding my step dad John.

I believe with all of those thirty-eight long years of being a police officer and wearing the radio by the right side of his shoulder, my step dad John and another police officer he worked with developed a rare cancer on the right side of their necks: parotid gland cancer. It was removed, and many rounds of chemo and radiation seemed to have done the trick, until the cancer spread to his lungs then spread to the bones and then under the skin.

Every time we thought he was getting better he would go for another scan, and a new type of cancer would appear somewhere else. I was obsessed with trying to save him. I felt I was different and I would be able to find this magical cure to cancer. Still, deep down inside I knew this was what was going to take him from us. My soul knew something my heart just couldn't accept.

The lights of the Angels will guide you home, but first I will try to fix you.

The first thing I did when I found out this disease was plaguing us was to run straight to the store and buy him a card with words of encouragement. I strongly felt his mother's spirit and I told him that although his mom passed from cancer, she wasn't calling his name to be up there with her right now. She was going to be with him during this difficult time. John loved and cared for his mother, she lived directly across the street from him. They were very close, one of the only times I saw my step dad cry was at her funeral. So, I gave my step dad this beautiful little lamp of the blessed Mother Mary. It belonged to his mother, and when she passed away many years ago, I helped clean out her house with him. He was so shocked I still had it! Seriously though, this devoted woman could have opened a Catholic gift shop with all of the religious items she had. I swear she never missed a Sunday at church either! When we were cleaning the bedrooms, we laughed with each other and made the sign of the Cross, asking God to forgive us when we had to throw away some of the plastic rosaries she had: there were bags and bags filled with them. I was like, "shouldn't we just drop them back off at the doorsteps at church?" That's when he said, "If you want to keep something that's fine, pick one thing, so I did, and it was that beautiful little lamp of the blessed Mother Mary holding roses. That item meant so much to me, and I know it meant so much to John when I gave it to him during that most difficult battle of cancer.

I went to the holistic store and bought raw honey, turmeric, and frankincense, because I read about their benefits. We would sit at the kitchen table together and John would use the raw honey for his oatmeal and take shots of the turmeric and rub the frankincense on his neck. I look back and I literally had him try anything I walked through the door with! I read about a guy in Southern Illinois who won his battle with cancer using RSO cannabis oil, so I contemplated getting some from Colorado. So you better believe I found a way to smuggle that into our state! I didn't care about those laws at that time. We luckily have dispensaries all over the place here now in Illinois.

I was now John's nurse; he would call me his nurse. My first dad used to call me that, but just so I would massage his back. When my step dad said it, it was genuine and loving and with a sense of pride. If I noticed he wasn't feeling well from chemo, I would go to the local soup lady and drop off soup, by the back door. I once left him a St. Jude pendant by the door, and for weeks he never knew it was from me! I tried everything!

I literally wrote out a care plan and medicine schedule on med sheets from my work. We were desperate to make anything work, but I think our souls knew how this was going to end. I still fought whatever my spirit guides showed me at that time, because I was so invested in changing his destiny. I was trying to control everything. I know I wasn't the only one. I saw my step dad struggling, but I never saw him giving up. I respected that so much. He literally lost function in his right arm from the cancer spreading and radiation treatments—and yet he still got up every single day like clockwork and made his oatmeal and worked out. He was fearless and nothing ever stopped this strong man of ours!

About six to nine months before his passing, I had a dream that I was in the hospice room. I could see certain people there and what they were wearing. I then walked up to my step dad, but I could only hug him from around his waist because he was hooked up to machines. He was dying and there was nothing I could do but say goodbye and hug him one last time.

Well, months went by, and I started to avoid my step dad John. I just knew what was coming, and I couldn't look him in the eyes because of what my guides showed me in that dream. He would ask me to go to lunch, and I would make excuses, even though I really wanted to go. He would ask me to stop by, but I had other things to do. I was scared. I just wanted his illness to be going better, but it wasn't. I was avoiding death, yet I didn't want to avoid him. Then the lights started to go out and tv's would shut on and off at my house, and the kids' toys would go off again. I felt it was my Aunt Gigi showing up again to let me know everything was going to be okay, but my emotions just kept taking over, and I just kept crying when I was alone and when I was driving in the car. The spiritual awakening was coming and I fought it like a bad storm!

This had been happening to me since I was a young child, yet I didn't know who to go to for help.

I saw John last on a Tuesday afternoon. I could see the look in his eyes, that same look I saw when I witnessed his mother last before she passed from cancer. He was so skinny, and his neck had some red bloody blotchy areas because of the tumors coming up from the skin. I'm a nurse, so why did seeing this bother me so much? I should be able to handle all of this, but I just couldn't see him like that. I just cried.

My Mom and my step dad stopped by to hide my brother's car in my garage. They had to steal it because he was in a psychosis manic state and went off his meds. My brother found a vacant house under construction. The owner was a truck driver, so he was out of town, and my brother made his way into his house and started wearing that guy's boots and clothes as if they were his. My mom had seen him with these new clothes, but he told her he got a construction job. So again she didn't think anything of it. Shock occurred when the man of the house came home to find my brother asleep in his bed. I don't know if this benefited my brother or not, but the homeowner became aware of my brother's mental illness, so he didn't press charges after all of his items were returned. So my mother and I, as well as my step dad, decided my brother shouldn't have a car, so we hid it in my garage. When they pulled away, I knew that was going to be the last time I saw John. Up until this day, I still live with so much regret that I didn't hug and kiss him one last time. I was so upset with our hardships spiraling out of control, like my brother's mental status and John's progressing cancer. I felt defeated once again, and so did my mother.

On that crisp January day I just kept pacing the sidewalk back and forth; I said to God, "if you're going to take him [John], you better make it quick and peaceful." I don't know why, but I asked my hospice patient Phil to come get him and help him cross over. Phil reminded me of my step dad in the way he would love and care for his wife. I wanted Phil to show my step dad the way I took care of him in hospice and that I was a good nurse; for so many reasons that was just so hard to do for my step dad because his pain was my pain. I had to accept that I wasn't his nurse in those moments I was his step daughter. He was a part of my Soul Group: watching him go was one of the hardest tasks of my life. The next day at the doctor's office, they were given the grim news from John's oncologists, who did everything possible, but the cancer had spread to his bones. Time to prepare for hospice. My step dad had a cough and fluid in his lungs, but the doctor sent him home anyway. My mom said she doesn't know how she made it home because of all the tears she cried. My step dad John sat in the passenger seat in shock; all he thought about was my mom. Brushing her tears from her face, he said "I knew I loved you from the first time I saw you." My mom sobbed; good-hearted John was trying to comfort her. He saw how broken she was knowing they soon would part.

Still trying so hard to control the situation, I begged my mom to take him back to the hospital or even a different hospital to get the fluid drained, but the doctor told them they could drain it on Monday. That made no sense to me. I told her he could end up in the ICU this weekend, but of course nobody listened to me. I just cried and cried. I remember stepping outside in the deep freezing cold to catch my breath. I reminded myself to just breathe in and out. I felt the walls caving in on me.

> *"Tears are words that need to be written."*
> *– Paulo Coehlo*

I have this gift, and I was trying to help, but I couldn't get through with my message; my loved ones just weren't listening.

The next morning I talked to my step dad on the phone. I told him I understood why God wanted to take him: he came here to serve and protect, and he had done it. Even the way he took care of animals, he displayed compassion and care. Actually, my step dad lived right around the block from us as kids, and we knew him. Everyone knew the policeman with the big white dog named Nika. She was always walked and well-fed with fresh turkey meat from the deli. We called her "the never-ending story dog." My step dad let us pet her. We would often walk around the block to check if she were outside, hoping to pet her from the gate.

I explained to John how he was the best "second" dad ever and that I loved him so much, that he did an amazing job here on earth during his lifetime, and that he served his life's path and purpose well. I loved him for the way he loved his own mother and adored her. I told him how proud he made her by the way he would love and take care of his brothers and his family. Most importantly for truly loving my mother, even for the way he would move her curly hair out of her face and kiss her. To witness our mother being loved so completely was so important for us kids to witness. I told John how good he was to me for taking me to get my driver's license, and how when we pulled up in his flashy Audi, he told me to tell the instructor that car was my birthday present, just so we could get a good laugh out of the guy. I told him thank you for always being so calm and making me feel so safe driving in cars. Led Zeppelin songs always reminded me of our car rides together, especially their one song called "Going to California". I thanked him for everything he did for me and my mom and for all he did for others in his lifetime. As you might imagine, our lifetime together was flashing before me; I even thanked him for that one time he picked me up from camp when I caught lice!

Every Valentine's Day, John would send my mother a bouquet of her favorite color roses, purple, and he would send me and my sisters a single rose each. He would give me cards for every special occasion. I thanked him for the time he put jumper cables in my car and got me my first cell phone so that I had some kind of communication device on me. I still have those jumper cables he put in my first car, and my cell phone is still the same number. How naturally he knew how to be a loving father.

John was an avid movie buff. Every Tuesday he would make his way to Best Buy for the new dvd's. One of his favorite movies and quotes was from *The Last Samurai,* so I left it with that quote. I will miss our conversations. The last phone call was the hardest and saddest conversation: all he said to me was, "April, I don't want to go." Hearing those words broke my heart. Right after that, he panicked and said, "I gotta go, I need to hang up," and so he did. I just cried: how could the strongest yet kindest man I know be going? My heart shattered to pieces in that moment because I knew that was our last conversation. There was nothing I could have done for him. I felt so helpless.

> *"Our lives become a parchment, our sufferings and our actions are the ink. The workings of the Holy Spirit are the pen, and with it God writes a living Gospel."*
> *– Jean-Pierre de Caussade*

That night John collapsed at home: the fluids filled up his lungs. I didn't find out until days later that this occurred. I was devastated. I didn't blame my mother, but I think she avoided calling me. I told her what was going to happen and begged her to take him to the hospital. His collapse was just like my dream, and it happened no matter what I tried to do. At this point, I couldn't control my emotions. I suffered a spiritual awakening and nervous breakdown all at once.

Many police officers came to say goodbye to him at the hospital, probably hundreds of them.

My step dad was on a ventilator for about a week until right when they decided to take him off. He seemed to be doing better. Once he was off the ventilator, he was supposed to be moved out of the ICU. So, almost everyone thought they could go home and get something to eat; my mom went for a shower and change of clothes. That's when one of my siblings mentioned to John, "Okay, mom is gone; she went home." He looked to the left and right to scan the room to make sure, and that's when he took his last breath. I've seen this before with many of my other patients. Patients wait for their loved ones to leave the room. They hold on for them for so long, unable to pass in front of them. Their bond was just so strong, and that is what kept him alive, but it was his time to go. I feel that my mom needed to leave to take care of herself for him to transition to the other side. Unfortunately, my mom still lives with that regret to this day—that she could not be there every single moment—and that the one "second" she left, he decided to pass.

CHAPTER FOURTEEN:

Grief

> *The death of any loved parent is an incalculable lasting blow. Because no one ever loves you again like that.*
> *– Brenda Ueland*

After my step dad's passing, I was unable to eat or sleep. All I did was cry. I would look at my beautiful children and feel so bad because I was in so much pain, yet so numb: in a dark hole of an existence—meanwhile everything continued to go on around me. I felt left behind; I was drowning inside. I felt like I didn't belong in this world; everything was just so dark to me. Nobody had heard from me in weeks because I stopped answering my phone. Unknowingly, I was busy exploring the depths of my soul and at the same time, trying to understand mysteries of the universe and the other side. I was in such a spiritual war with myself, having forgotten that the connection to the Divine was my greatest "weapon".

That inner voice from my childhood started speaking to me again and although I was so scared, my soul recognized it. Spirit was telling me to just listen and be still. Death isn't meant to hurt or break us but to let the light in; we must trust there is more to life than this. Such insights represent a spiritual awakening. I was receiving just too much energy at that moment; I just wanted to curl up into a ball, yet be held at the same time. The spirit world has been trying to awaken me since I was a child. I was in such deep grief, and so were many others around me. I felt their pain along with mine. People would wonder why I didn't go to see John to say goodbye or why I didn't go to the memorial. I was in my car all ready, but I just couldn't stop crying; I felt angry the world was going on while my entire world had stopped turning. I was just so broken inside. I looked up and one of the local police officers tapped on my car window. I saw his badge covered in a black stripe in memory of my step dad; I just started crying even more to know he was honored. This officer said he would help me walk into the memorial if I wanted his help and not to go through this alone. I was grateful for his kind words, but I just couldn't; I wanted to go back to bed and wake up when this grief was all over! Like a little girl, I wanted my mom, too, but she was so heartbroken as well. People were talking about the way I was handling my grief—as if I was doing it wrong!

"If you are never alone, you cannot know yourself.
And if you do not know yourself, you will begin
to fear the void"
– Rumi

By the way, there is no wrong way to grieve: no damn handbook exists for this thing called life and its encounters with death. If you're grieving, be gentle with yourself. Don't pay attention to any time frame, either. Grief is the last act of love we have to give to those we loved. Where there is deep grief, there was great love.

I had great love for my step dad: he was the greatest man of my life. If you simply cannot understand why someone is grieving so much, for so long, consider yourself fortunate you do not understand. For me, no one could compare to him.

In the mornings I would get up and have to peel myself out of bed just to put my son on the bus for school, and then I would come back upstairs with Cheerios and put on "My Little Pony" for my daughter and just climb right back into bed: the song from that haunted me over and over, "My Little Pony and Friends": I felt like I was in the Twilight Zone.

My gifts and my experiences meant I was not limited to grief. But regret still was present since I could never shake feeling responsible for knowing my step dad's fate prior to his death.

Disney's *Coco* came out then, and my kids loved it. It's a beautiful movie about Dia de Los Muertos, the Day of the Dead, and all the souls who crossover. With that movie came the theme song, "Remember Me": "though I have to say good-bye, remember me; don't let it make you cry, even though I know how very far apart we are, you'll be in my arms again; remember me." Again I cried: that song seemed to provide yet another message from the other side. Those lyrics sure are empowering.

The winter of John's passing was just so cold and dark, and I felt like I was in a dream. I wasn't sleeping much, so my nerves were pretty much shot, to the point that my head was buzzing. I would take showers constantly to help me calm down, but nothing seemed to work. I couldn't bear to see him like that at the hospital; I couldn't bear to attend his memorial, so of course regret had dug its nails into me.

I was a complete hot mess. I passed my hardest moments alone, trying to convince everyone I was fine, when indeed, I was not. I probably should have gone to the doctor: this was no doubt a nervous breakdown, yet my soul was on fire. I was in such deep grief I could barely leave my house. I feared my grief would resonate with others and burden them with my sadness. I didn't want to burden anyone, so I just stayed home.

I also noticed that, after my step dad's passing, I felt completely abandoned, but to make up for that feeling, I started helping people and going out of my way for others, even when they didn't offer one ounce of kindness back to me. I was so vulnerable. Some people chose to take advantage of that. But the truth is I was never abandoned; grief just led me to believe that. I had to start standing up for myself once again. I had to heal from trauma from my childhood that crept up on me once again. My step dad didn't abandon me: he loved me. Now abandonment issues had been triggered, but John was certainly not to blame...

Thankfully, over time, I would go for walks and be saved by my children. I made my way throughout the neighborhood without the fear of my grief wreaking havoc onto others. I pushed through the pain by sitting with the beauty of the sunlight and the moonlight. Nature and the spirit of my children helped me heal.

Please remember to be gentle with yourself during times of grief. I promise you the light will shine again. When so much crumbles around you, you are making space for more light to enter. Trust this! Often the deepest pain empowers you to grow into your highest self!

When I would finally fall asleep at night, all of a sudden, I would feel a poke at my feet, and I would jolt awake. I knew it was my step dad. I told him, "I'm so sorry you didn't make it; you passed from this stupid cancer. The treatments didn't work, but if you can please come to me in my dreams, do so, because right now I can't even eat or sleep or think straight since I miss you so much." I was in between two worlds. Within days after asking, he sure did deliver. That's when I had my first dream about him coming to me and telling me about my sister being sick and showing me he was safe and okay (see 1st chapter above).

One early morning I was between wakefulness and sleep and I clearly heard my name being called right to my face! So loud and clear" "APRIL!" I pulled the covers over my head and thought "oh my God, am I really going crazy!" I thought I was going to be a diagnosed schizophrenic like my brother. I recognized that voice, though, calling "APRIL": I know in my heart and soul it was my Aunt Gigi, still with me making my kids' toys go off again. I swear the door to the other side was blown right open for me, but I was so scared.

I then started to find old graduation and birthday cards from twenty years ago from my step dad. These served as signs he was talking to me through these cards: some even read, "Happy little SIGNS of Life", to confirm what I experienced were "signs" from him and indeed true. He was sending me so many signs—from feathers to heart-shaped clouds in the sky! I finally answered the phone for my high school friend Savana, the one I shared so many ESP moments with in high school. I saw her phone call and thought if anyone is going to understand the phenomenon I continue to experience, she for sure would! She cried with me and sent me a picture of a rainbow outside of her window! We both knew that was a sign! A Rainbow in January, in Chicago, that normally just doesn't exist!

One card I found from John said, "All that knowledge shoved into your head… And it didn't explode! Now that's something you can be proud of!" Those sweet gestures were typical of him prior to his passing. He confirmed my entire life connected to the Angels and life on the other side does exist! Another card depicts a little animal answering a phone; it says, "ring ring Happy Birthday," and inside it says, "IT'S FOR YOU!" His death truly was not meant to hurt me, but to awaken my soul.

My step dad gave me a card for helping him clean out his mother's house after her passing: "THANK YOU APRIL; Thanks for all your help!" I so needed to hear this once again. I tried so damn hard to save him and be his little nurse. I also found a card a few months later right after my birthday. It had a little snail on it: "Slow but sure, Happy Birthday a little late." He never missed my birthdays! He modelled so much love.

All of these cards validated my spiritual awakening to his spirit. They helped complete things left unsaid. I never physically got myself to say goodbye, but I know finding these cards provided just what I needed to move forward during the times of grief ahead.

Remember how I asked my hospice patient Phil to come greet him and help him transition? Well, I came across Phil's Mass Prayer Card a few days after my step dad's passing, and I knew in that moment they were on the other side showing me my prayers were answered!

The grieving process was so intense, yet receiving all of these signs presented me with so much meaning—and convinced me John was trying to get a hold of me to say all the things left unsaid.

My step dad would continue to visit me in dreams. Remember, I once told him, "If anything ever happens to you, come to me, and I will let mom know." He would tell me things, like that my mom's car needed to be serviced. When I told my mom that very message, she responded, "Oh my service light just came on in my car." Or he would come to me in my dream and say, "Make sure you tell your mother she looks beautiful!" And when I would wake up to call and tell my mom, she would often say she had a dream the same night with him in it as well, but could not recall any details. So basically, I was the "middle man" for them.

One time in my dream, my mom was missing something, and John was telling she should look by the dresser, so I called her and hinted that if she should be missing anything, she should look by the dresser. She was actually searching all over for their wedding pictures but couldn't find them, so I just said, "Well, whatever you're missing, John said to look by the dresser." One day after that, she was reading the Sunday newspaper and needed her reading glasses, and when she went into the bedroom, she looked all over for them. Yes even by the dresser, but they weren't there. As she was leaving the bedroom, the TV turned on! She turned it off and went to leave, and the TV turned back on again! When she went to turn it off a second time, she saw her reading glasses on the floor by the dresser! She called me thinking she was going crazy and told me not to put this on Facebook. (I laughed to think I might put it in a book instead!")

We are energy, energy never dies, it just changes form.

The night of my mom's first birthday without John physically here, he finally came to her in a dream. She was running up to him outside while he was walking up the driveway; she just kept hugging and kissing him, telling him how much she missed him. He responded, "What do you mean, I've been right here!" My mom was so relieved to have had a visitation and connection of her own! John NEVER missed a birthday, so what a great gift for her that was.

It took my mom a couple of months to return to work after John's passing. She was very hesitant to return because the grief was so thick and heavy on her heart and soul. She was sitting in the parking lot at work, contemplating whether or not to go inside. She was scrolling through old voicemails on her phone. She landed on one of John's old messages saying, "Hey Hun, I'm here." This validated his spirit with her in that moment and gave her the courage to go inside.

Then on my birthday my mom stopped by and while leaving my house, she heard my daughter Mariah say, "Oh hurry up gramma, grandpa is in the car waiting for you!"

Another time, my step dad John came to me in yet another dream and was concerned about my mom: he said, "I don't know why she's so sad and not taking care of herself; I'm sitting right here on the couch next to her... Plus she forgets to lock the front door; allowing anyone to walk right in." So the next day I called my mom to tell her about my dream, and she said last night while watching TV she left the door unlocked and my brother just walked right in. He was in one of his manic phases; mom was so nervous she almost called an ambulance for help. John's spirit must have seen this and chose me once again to remind my mother to be mindful of her surroundings. He wanted me to urge her to care more for herself and not allow his death to cripple her life with such deep grief. Our loved ones truly are always with us. Spouses take a vow, "Til Death do us part," but their care for us extends even beyond death.

My mom would always say how each sunrise was so hard for her; for me it was another sunset...another day that went by without your physical spirit here on earth—and yet receiving all these signs made the physical world a bit more spiritually sweeter.

In these moments my gifts created the perfect storm: a Spiritual awakening. I had experiences with my children in the car, memories of being in a car accident as a child crept back up on me, grief for my step dad dying, thus losing the person who had become a safe haven for me, and pain for my brother's illness breaking the hearts of our family.

I'm not sure why I was given these abilities, but I remain amazed when I am provided such specific information and Downloads from the other side. I feel that, once I had kids and the loss of my step dad, my senses got stronger and blew open the doors to the other side. I tried to keep them closed most of my life, but that holding-in made me so anxious. I had to start being true to myself, the trust of my step dad coming through helped me along the way.

"Our real reality is beyond the five senses."
– Deepak Chopra

CHAPTER FIFTEEN:

Knockin' on Heaven's Door

I am convinced our loved ones on the other side are not locked up in Heaven and that we are their "heaven." I was shown once again what the inside of Heaven was like, and it's truly right here with us. Loved ones are beside us every single day; they can still love us unconditionally, warn us, and protect us.

I started to journal because a co-worker, a strict Christian lady, gave me a journal after my step dad's passing. She wanted me to follow the path of Jesus and join her church. But I knew what she hoped with her sweet gesture wouldn't mesh with my gifts and abilities. Many times she dismissed psychic mediums and even expressed how God turns His back on those who seek people with such abilities. She felt such supernatural meddling was the devil's work; nevertheless, I took her present and started to journal daily. With gratitude, I would think of my step dad and my Aunt Gigi, acknowledging all the things they taught me in this lifetime. I also came across an old journal from elementary school with Mr. Z's handwriting and the message, "Journal more throughout your life!" I found out he too had passed away: I knew this was a strong sign from him to transfer my pain into writing and healing.

Gratitude is an emotion you feel, but also a form of guidance. It encourages you to consider how special life is. It helps you to focus positively on what you have—not on what you lack.

More and more signs started to show up, like feathers, and toys started going off again. I also heard Led Zeppelin songs when I was thinking of my step dad; sometimes the music app on my phone would jump on by itself and play our favorite Zeppelin songs, like "Going to California." Signs like this suggested he knew I would talk to him in my writing and he was receiving the communications. I then started to see hawks in the sky, great Messengers from above from our Spirit guides, our past loved ones, and the divine. Little did my sweet Christian co-worker know or understand that I too am gifted and can receive messages from The Messenger to help heal others, just like her adoring Jesus and other significant saints and healers. God gave his gifts to us all, remember that.

Religion is following the messenger; spirituality is following the message!

You see, someone like my step dad wasn't just the "average Joe", he was a very evolved soul, meaning his consciousness was elevated due to the way he served his path and purposes here on earth. His strong soul was able to show signs like these right away. I am also so open to the other side; I was just a vessel and able to relay the messages from him and others—a little bit more clearer than most. So please, don't beat yourself up over trying to connect with the other side. Be patient but at the same time be open to receiving the signs as well.

He even came to my cousin while she was on Spring Break in Mexico with her friends. They were all sitting around the pool and they started talking about dreams. Her friend said she recently had a weird dream about her childhood friend's Dad. My cousin asked who the man was, and she said my step dad's first and last name. My cousin's mouth dropped. She said, "That's my aunt's husband and he literally just passed away in January a few months ago." Her friend said in her dream she walked into his house and he was sitting at the kitchen table just smiling away.

I know the other side can see who we are all connected to and how to send a message. He chose that opportunity once again to prove he was okay and smiling away! I'm convinced that at night when we go to sleep sometimes we wake up in Heaven!

"Standin' on a hill in the mountain of dreams tellin' myself it's not as Hard, Hard, Hard as it seems."
"Going to California"
– LED ZEPPELIN

CHAPTER SIXTEEN:

You're Not Sick; You're Psychic!

I started to dream again about death. I dreamed my friend's dog died, that it was sick and laying helpless, unable to move. A few days later on Facebook that friend posted her beloved dog died. I also dreamt of my friend's dad who I'd seen on Facebook, that he died, and then he did. Then I dreamt about a friend's husband down in Florida. In my dream he had a cancer scare but was walking along the beach joking with everyone about how he was going to be alright. I kind of felt like he was celebrating. I heard him say, "If God brought me to it, God will see me through it" I messaged my friend and said, "I don't really know your husband and I don't want to scare you, but I had this dream…" So I told her what I saw. She was shocked and scared because her husband has a mole on his face that planned to get checked out, but hadn't yet had the courage to do so. They were nervous he would develop the same skin cancer his father had. For peace of mind I encouraged her to have the doctor examine him. I then followed up with her to learn great news that his biopsy was benign.

These premonitions were still very overwhelming for me. I didn't know how to make this stop. I felt cursed. Again nobody heard from me in weeks because I just stopped answering the phone. I was in a commitment with solitude; I had to become best friends with my soul again. At night time, those faces of the people from the other side started to line up again. One by one, they stood there, loved ones from all over the world, all over Heaven. Heaven was calling me again. No matter how tight I would shut my eyes, as soon as I opened them, those Angel's faces were still there. I sensed my time had come to do this service for others. The spirits, people's loved ones, woke me up. I remember looking outside my window one night, saying to the universe and the bright full moon, "Fine! If you really want me to do this, and if this is truly a part of my Soul's Life path and purpose, I'm in! I just don't want to see death anymore. I don't want the overwhelming feeling of responsibility. I also want to go back to my normal life with my children for just a little bit longer, but I will do this for all inside of Heaven. Just send me the utmost right genuine people to help me along this lonely path." So my sweet Angels listened to my list of demands.

"For there is always light, if only we're brave enough to see it. If only we're brave enough to be it."
– Amanda Gorman

A few months prior to my step dad's death, I had a medium come over. I told her how I was experiencing spiritual things, and she told me I was basically a psychic medium and that I would develop very fast. She thankfully added me to some groups on Facebook, and I said to myself, I need a mentor like that lady who helped the Long Island Medium on the tv show on TLC. She experienced the same anxieties and phobias I did before she understood and accepted her gifts. I put that out to the universe, and through a string of synchronicities within days we were connected! I saw on Facebook that she, Pat Longo, was going to be on a podcast radio show called "Evolving Soul", together with another well-known psychic medium Anthony Mrocka, so I listened in.

Pat Longo is an author and an internationally known healer and spiritual mentor. After listening, I listened in again on one of her spiritual awareness courses. I was so happy to be able to join her online classes named after her book, (who most people refer to as the spiritual Bible) *The Gifts Beneath Your Anxiety*. Pat literally went down a list of symptoms and occurrences I was experiencing, like the ringing in the ears, and the lights and TV's going on and off, the tingling feelings in my body, and other anxious feelings I had since I was a kid. She talked about the way I would see shadows and sparkles and have premonitions. I then contacted her, and we booked a session together.

No need for a medical solution: this was a spiritual need! Someone had finally called the doctor, but this time a spiritual one!

The first thing Pat said to me was, "You're not sick; you're psychic!" She indicated I had been suppressing my gifts and that was causing the anxiety. She told me I had God-given gifts and I had an extremely heightened sense of intuition: that I was, in fact, a gifted psychic medium. This identity meant I could communicate with and receive messages from beings in the spirit world. So I wasn't crazy! Ladies and gentlemen, let me tell ya, I was relieved! My time had come to start using these gifts and no longer ignore them. They were very strong. Pat then did a healing session and balanced out my chakras and helped me understand my abilities and gifts. Pat also told me to start writing signs down and establish dates when I started to feel things around certain people, so I did. I also joined spirit circles weekly online with wonderful teachers who, once again, appeared by the grace of God to help expand these gifts. Spirit circles are circles with like-minded people like myself who have these gifts and abilities to practice with one another. People from the West to the East Coast and countries all over the world! Psychic medium Anthony Mrocka as well as Pat Longo hosted a few of these online spirit circles. This gave me the opportunity to meet so many amazing gifted people to help me feel so welcome. We would laugh and jokingly refer to our community as the "Harry Potter Academy."

Pat also told me the importance of meditation—of grounding oneself every day, so I started to meditate outside (by then it was summertime). I started to feel more at ease about my step dad's passing, and insights started to come to me about his death. I realized, while in meditation, that I'm not angry anymore at the doctors for letting him go home with fluid in his lungs; I understood that decision was actually all part of God's plan. But I seemingly took forever to get to the point of acceptance. God's last gift to John was to listen to all the people who came near and far to let him know how much he impacted their lives. He was such a humble man; he wouldn't have listened to his praises while still verbal. He had to be quiet. I sent a text message to my mom about my epiphany, and as soon as I did that, I saw a hawk in the sky—and a rainbow. These signs allowed me a perfect beautiful moment, quite the validation of my gifts and our connection. The moment was so beautiful and I was so amazed, as if I had seen unicorns and dragons flying through the sky. At that moment I was healing myself. I also realized we can outwardly pray to God and He will listen, but by going within through meditation, God answers!

I always tell my mom I would walk through hell again, go through all my childhood traumas again, knowing those experiences would lead to my step dad.

When my half-sister called me to send her condolences, I told her to make sure she tells my biological dad thank you for never reaching out to me or ever trying to reconnect: someone better came along to take his place and for that I am ever so grateful and he is forgiven.

I know with everything I have overcome, God can now send me people who need to hear my story so I can help heal them during our sessions. I truly believe people must go through tough circumstances which almost destroy them, so they can figure out who they really are. In my case: I was born to be...a medium!

As indicated, I believe we have these Soul Groups, and people come here to be a part of our lives and part of our plan. My step dad was a big part of my life in many ways. He helped me after my childhood trauma; he played a big part in who I became growing up—and his illness and passing became a big part of my spiritual awakening—of my development and growth as a medium.

> *"Prayer is talking to God, Meditation is listening."*
> *– Pat Longo, Spiritual Healer*

Pat also mentioned she wouldn't be surprised that he signed up to be my guide. I truly believe he did! He used to say things to me when he was alive that didn't make sense until now. When I would stop by the house, John would always ask me where I was out and where I might go next. He would say, "Where are you on to next on The Pony Express!" I never wanted to offend him and his old (corny) expressions. After his passing, I looked up the meaning of The Pony Express, and of course the phrase was all about delivering messages back in the 1860's. I feel our souls in this life were always meant to be part of one another allowing us to serve healing messages to others. I think that, before we got here, my step dad agreed to a pact to get me back on track to this path and purpose—no matter the circumstances or cost. Everything sure did feel impossible right before a massive change took place, but I got through the pain.

CHAPTER SEVENTEEN:

Behind the Veil

By this time my family thought I was crazy, and I was pretty much labeled the black sheep of the family. They even plotted to have me committed because they thought maybe I was going to end up like my brother. Instead, I was learning how to ground and surround myself with protection and to set boundaries with the other side to help eliminate the anxiety. Pat Longo gave me great spiritual tools for that. Everyday, I got up and I would put my feet on the ground and envision three cords of white light, one from the bottom of my tailbone, and two from my feet, all going into the ground like the roots of a cherry blossom tree. Then, I would surround myself with a bubble of God's white light of protection, and lastly I'd picture a shield of armor like St Michael's, to protect me from negative thoughts and negative beings. I started to feel better every single day, and I would make sure to set aside time to meditate weekly. I used sage in my house, as well, quite frequently, as I started to connect with Spirit more and more. I even jokingly gave myself the name "Secret Psychic", and I hid my abilities for quite some time before slowly coming out to family and friends.

Many more people are going to discover my gifts and abilities once I release this book! So allow me to reintroduce myself! I am April: a psychic medium. I would literally hide upstairs in the bathroom and give readings. I had to have my sitters write me emails after each reading to say what their experience was like, so that I could collect evidence to prove to my family that I was not crazy! Yes, now you know that usually the black sheep of the family is telling the truth; we see the world differently than others, because we are pretty much between two worlds. I was born this way; God makes no mistakes, and this was my birthright. The reason I was having such a hard time trusting my intuition is because I was so convinced that some outsiders knew better than me. Deep intuition is the navigation of your soul. Only you can find the way by going within. *Follow your soul. It knows the way!*

> *"You always had the power my dear,*
> *you just had to learn it for yourself."*
> ***Glinda The Good Witch***
> *– The Wizard Of OZ.*

CHAPTER EIGHTEEN:

Veterans

To be honest, I still struggled to accept my gifts, but I continued to write things down about people as Pat said I should, and then, of course, I asked my brother-in-law permission if I could tell him what I saw around him. I saw a young man standing in uniform. He kept coming to me, someone who served tours in Iraq with my brother-in-law. After 9-11 he took his own life due to PTSD related issues from the war. I asked my brother-in-law if he knew a soldier like that, and he said yes. My voice was shaking. I paced back and forth. This was confirmation I could channel the other side. I knew he'd been gone for awhile because he had been coming to me for months. My brother-in-law confirmed he passed in October of the previous year, but just learned this week of early July about his death. His deceased friend wanted me to provide some healing messages for my brother-in-law: to tell him he knows he works with veterans to this day and helps so many vets like him with their needs and benefits. "Tell him to continue to do so even when he feels like there is no hope; he makes a difference." I also saw rows of soldiers lining up on the other side saluting him.

My brother-in-law confirmed these feelings and how deeply he needed this message: he dealt with major PTSD after the war, and he felt veterans like him get left in the shadows to figure things out for themselves, never really honored or cared for. The result is an epidemic of veteran suicides due to PTSD from war zone experiences. This has been going on for too many years, from many different times of war. We as a country don't take care of these fellow protectors. My brother-in-law is doing amazing: he's such a loving husband and father to his children. Going to war at such a young age was such a bittersweet experience for him. I believe his friend wanted to make sure he knew the important path he currently follows.

"Out of suffering have emerged the strongest souls; the most massive characters are seared with scars."
– Khalil Gibran

Veterans Hotline: 1-800-273-8255.

CHAPTER NINETEEN:

My Sister's Best Friend's Wedding

I was on the phone with one of my many sisters, who like most of my siblings I consider gifted as well. I basically came out of the "psychic closet" to her. She was so accepting of what I revealed to her and really listened to the things happening to me. I felt safe talking about my abilities; I'm convinced she shares similar gifts. She had to cut me short, because she was going to dinner with her friend Gianna; I suddenly felt the urge to tell her that when she sees Gianna, she should let her know her mom knows about the bouquet for her wedding. Quietly at the table, my sister did convey the message. Gianna's eyes lit up; my sister then said, "Text April if you would like to talk to her." A few days later, Gianna and I were on the phone and her mom was with us both. She wanted Gianna to know that, on her wedding day, she knew Gianna suffered since she could not be with her in person, but she sure was there in Spirit. Gianna's mom said she knew she took her special handkerchief and wrapped it around her bouquet, so that she could be with her as she walked down the aisle. Only Gianna and her bridal party knew about the handkerchief! Her mother also wanted her to know she approves of the man she married, and that, when they have children, she will be with her.

Gianna's mom also wanted her to know that she's always in the car with her just like when here in the physical world, but that Gianna wasn't paying enough attention to the signs. So she said, "Tell her I was with her when she bought the shiny visor clip the other day for her car." Gianna had not told anyone, not even her husband, that she felt her mother's spirit and the need to buy this metal shiny visor item she found at Hobby Lobby. On it is written "Faith will guide you through."

Gianna's mom was a bit religious, not one, in life, to ever embrace some type of mediumship like this. She was more quiet and reserved, but she used me that day as a vessel to let her daughter know she was there with her, and she wanted her to move forward in life and to stop replaying over and over in her head the day she died in front of her. She wanted her to know that her time had come to pass on, and that she was so sorry she died in front of her. Gianna's grandma also died in front of her mom, so that was not the way she wanted to go. Gianna's mom collapsed one cold winter night, and Gianna vigorously performed CPR on her mother, but neither her nor the paramedics could save her. Gianna was so lost and slipped into a very deep depression after her mother's passing; they were very close. Gianna kept saying, "April, that time was so bad, and I mean bad." She sought therapy and medication, but nothing seemed to help—that is until she had closure with her mother from our reading. Since then, Gianna has been able to understand; she says she can breathe a little easier since her healing session with me. She also gave birth to a beautiful baby girl and is doing such an amazing job creating many moments of love with her, the same way her mother did so with her.

We Are NEVER So Lost That
Our Angels Cannot Find Us!

CHAPTER TWENTY:

Cleaning Lady 819

One day I had a cleaning lady help me organize and clean my house, and immediately, I felt her father present. I told her about my abilities. By this time I was a bit more comfortable telling complete strangers, as opposed to people I knew from childhood. Anyway, I told her that her dad is here, saying he's sorry, but that he's okay and at peace. He left suddenly from a heart attack, and he was so sorry you didn't get to say goodbye. He's proud of you. Also, he knows you're going through a very hard time, and he keeps sending you signs by you finding dimes and change. She gasped and said, "Yes, I keep finding change in the oddest places; he would always help me out if I was struggling by giving me his change jar." Her father then showed me the number 8.19: she was shocked because that's her birthday. She was like, this is so weird, and I'm like, this is so weird, how am I getting such accurate things? I'm still just as in shock as the person receiving the messages from the other side! I was feeling confident in myself once again; this service was part of my heart and soul.

As we continued, I said to her, "Your father keeps showing me roses." She pulled up her sleeve and said she got a rose tattoo in memory of him because he was a gardener. She wanted his face, but he joked the rose was a better choice. He glowed like an angel now, but here on Earth, his face was far from that of an angel. We laughed; she teared up a bit: "Thank you so much, I wasn't even supposed to be here today. I was supposed to be on a bus back to Mexico." She had planned on taking her kids to her family's until she could get back on her feet and find them a place to live here. Her kids were actually waiting in the car while she was cleaning houses all that afternoon. Well, everything happens for a reason. Spirit has a funny way of showing up in times of need. We didn't finish organizing and cleaning, but I paid her the full amount for the day because I knew she needed it. Her father hinted my good deed would come back to me tenfold in so many different ways, and it truly has.

> *"The meaning of life is to find your gift.*
> *The purpose of life is to give it away."*
> *– Pablo Picasso*

CHAPTER TWENTY ONE:

KFC and
Watermelon

Dolly is a sweet woman from the South, with the sweetest twang in her voice. When I read for her, I saw her grandfather, strangely, with the KFC Colonel Sanders guy. She was in shock: her grandfather actually knew the KFC guy! He wanted her to know they were still good friends. Her grandfather was a painter back in the day and painted the very first KFC sign for that restaurant chain. He was never paid for it. He laughed and said to let Dolly know that, in heaven, all debts were forgiven. We thought that was a funny message! He also showed me how he loved the times they spent together when she was a child, sharing great conversations while snacking on watermelon. He then showed me a picture he cherished of her in her Easter dress, and Dolly confirmed they would often celebrate her birthday and Easter on the same day. Her grandfather showed me how sweet and loving he was to his wife and family, comparable to the movie *The Notebook*. Being so loved is all he ever wanted in this life. He now once again sent his love and was so grateful he was able to fulfill his wishes in his lifetime by building such a loving family.

CHAPTER TWENTY TWO:

1222 and Gold Coins

I had already given a few powerful readings, yet, I still couldn't believe that any of this was real. Naturally, I was still unsure of these abilities I now embrace as a gift, so I asked my guides to confirm once more that this is real. Our logical mind will often resist when Angels step in. I started to notice 12:22 in random places and on clocks. Then the date of 12/22 arrived. A friend open to my abilities informed me her friend would really like a reading. Her friend Mia sent me a picture of her grandfather, and immediately I felt his soul's spirit. He told me he had passed from Alzheimer's but also had many strokes and head injuries due to falls. Mia confirmed all this. He wanted her not to feel helpless anymore about his passing, that they made the right decision putting him in the nursing home. He was more of a father to her than her own father, who checked out of their relationship by succumbing to addictions or harmful self-medication. He wanted her to know to be taken care of by others became his last needed lesson here on earth. He also provided many lessons to the nursing staff and changed some of their lives, the way he changed Mia's. Some nurses never had a father figure, so they greatly benefitted from caring for someone with his gentle smile. Mia was so sad she wasn't left anything from her loving grandfather's belongings. I asked him to show me something he would have gotten her for a gift, since we were nearing Christmas-time. I was shown those chocolate gold coins that come in a little gold netted bag. Mia said her grandfather always, always handed those out to everyone for the holidays!

After our session, Mia revealed her dad called her with the news that he felt compelled to check her grandfather's safe. Inside that safe was an envelope with Mia's name on it, and inside were gold coins with the year she was born! Mia was so happy she had one last gift from her grandfather. What a special way of showing us this surprise during our reading! Spirit is intelligent; trust Spirit.

"We are not human beings having a spiritual experience.
We are spiritual beings having a human experience."
– Pierre Teilhard de Chardin

CHAPTER TWENTY THREE:

Missing Sister

I started to see Spirit more and more. Individual spirits look like their regular selves, yet more like a hologram version, if I had to describe them. Even when I would go outside for a walk and talk to my neighbor, there was her husband in his flannel standing next to her. They often would do the lawn work together, until he passed from Leukemia. I told Pat Longo how Spirit kept showing up and how I was expecting a friend over in a few days. I was so nervous because her sister was missing in another country; the incident even made the local news; I was afraid to say she was on the other side. Pat encouraged me to ask her permission when she arrived, so I did. Once my friend arrived, immediately, her sister was standing behind her. I got chills throughout my entire body. She wanted her sister to know that she was at her son's 16th birthday party, that she was around the family, and that she was thankful for everyone supporting her kids during this difficult time. She wanted her sister to know she loves her so much and was visiting her in dreams to help guide her.

My friend confirmed that she had been dreaming of her sister and that they just had her son's birthday party. She also feels her sister is no longer with us, because of how vivid her dreams are. The two were very close, and their connection is strong. She said, "It's like my heart and soul knows the answer, but, physically and mentally, I can't accept this." Although the case is ongoing, she wishes to cling to hope and faith that one day her sister will be found and that their family will be reunited.

CHAPTER TWENTY FOUR:

Tio's Horses and Abuela's Squirrel

Elena and I grew up with each other and had so many crazy fun times during our teenage years. She had a pool table, so all of us girls learned how to shoot pool together, so we could school the boys. When she turned 15, I stood up in her Quincenera. Elena and I kept in touch together over the years on social media; then she reached out to me for a reading. Once the reading started, I told her I saw a man, her Tio (uncle in Spanish). He was standing there with his beautiful show horses, stallions with braids and beautiful colors. He loved his horses and would often do big shows with them and win prizes. He then showed me the numbers 8-26, conveying a lot of happiness around them, but Elena didn't understand what they meant, so she called his daughter. Then started to cry because that was the date she gave birth to her first child. She wondered if her father knew about his first grandchild. He apologized and took responsibility for his passing, acknowledging that his drinking got out of hand. He wanted everyone to know he understands now what he should have done differently and that his soul was growing and evolving on the other side: he would always watch over them.

Then Elena's Abuela (grandma in Spanish) stepped forward. Right away she told me to tell Elena to have more patience with her daughter. The other day, while they were sitting on the couch, she brushed her hair way too hard! Elena laughed and said, "What a way to call me out, Abuela!" Abuela wanted her to know she has been setting the kids' toys off every so often to get her attention; she listens to her when she talks to her; nothing has changed. She wanted her to know she can walk again and even dance to salsa music whenever she wants! She then showed me the numbers 3-16, and she kept calling Elena's niece's name, wanting her to know she watches over her and refers to her as her "little muñeca", which is a doll in Spanish.

Elena knew those numbers corresponded to her niece's birth-day just last week; Abuela wanted her to know she was there and to send her Birthday wishes! She also had Elena's dogs with her in heaven and said she was feeding them table food. Abuela does whatever she wants! Then, all of a sudden, she showed me a squirrel. "Elena, why is your abuela showing me a squirrel, please tell me if I have this right." She was shocked. Elena said her Abuela went to Mexico and came back with a stuffed squirrel, because she loved it so much, and gave it to her daughter-in-law, Elena's mom, as a present. We could not stop laughing. I tuned in a little more because Abuela was picking something very specific to make sure Elena knew it was her; she wanted her to know she is with Elena's mom during this difficult time. Elena's mom is going through treatments for breast cancer and has been nervous about what lies ahead for her. Elena's Tio and Abuela wanted them to know that, although time goes by quickly here on Earth, that in Heaven, they don't have time, and that it doesn't exist. Our loved one's spirits truly are here with us and our families—forever until we meet again.

CHAPTER TWENTY FIVE:

Subway Foot Long Subs and Mom, Come Pick Me Up, I'm at the Police Station!

During my first official in-person reading, was I nervous? Yes, of course. I didn't know what to expect, but I had to surrender! This young boy Brian shows up with his mother. He brought a picture of his friend, hoping to connect with him. Right away, his friend told me he was about seventeen and died from an overdose. He apologized and took responsibility for his departure. He wanted Brian to know he shouldn't feel bad they lost touch with each other; he wanted him to stop holding on to the guilt he had for that. Brian started to cry. He felt so bad for not hanging out with him once his friend started to get into drugs. He thought if he would have stayed with him, maybe he would have never OD'd. Brian felt he could have led him on a better path. I then saw the logo for Subway over and over again; I didn't think anything of it, but I needed to remember, these signs were not about me. I had to surrender and trust Spirit to get whatever message across. So, I said to Brian, "What's with Subway, you know, the 5 foot-longs? I feel like this is a very funny situation, because your friend can't stop laughing." Brian then started to cry so much that his nose started to run. I had to run to the kitchen and get him some paper towels. I told him, "It's okay to cry, because those were tears of healing." He said, "No, I told my friend before we got here that if this was real, he better bring up the time we were being typical teenagers and ran away from the cops into the Subway restaurant to hide in the bathroom, but the manager snitched. So we were the only two who got arrested out of all the kids who ran." Brian laughed, and so did his mom, because she spent hours getting him out of the police station.

Brian felt so relieved his friend included that validating message. If I didn't bring that through, he wouldn't have been convinced his friend was the one sending messages. I have to say, if you plan to seek healing messages from a medium, I do not suggest you go about it this way; such targeted specifics do not always come through, and you will leave disappointed. However, that day was a powerful moment of healing. Oh, to be a punk teenager again!

CHAPTER TWENTY SIX:

Punky Brewster

Vanessa came to me hoping to connect with her mother. Vanessa didn't go out much since her mother's passing; if it wasn't for her children, she wouldn't have gotten out of bed most days. I could relate. Vanessa and her mother were inseparable, and being a single mother, Vanessa needed the extra love and support. Ever since her mother passed, she felt abandoned, because she lost a part of her heart and soul. Once we started the reading, her mother stood there with me and said, please tell my daughter I love her new hair do. Vanessa, with tears in her voice, said to me, I haven't gotten my hair done in a few years since my mother's passing, and I just did so last week. She wanted her daughter to know she was sorry her passing was sudden, and there were no goodbyes; she made sure to visit her in a dream after her passing to show her she was okay; she wanted to kiss and hug her good-bye one last time.

Vanessa confirmed she had the most beautiful vivid dream of her mother after her passing and that she was happy and said goodbye; kissed and hugged her tightly before hurrying off to her car, as if she was riding off to Heaven. She then told me to make sure Vanessa tells her sons to be careful playing baseball by the street. I then heard her say, "Punky Brewster." "OMG," Vanessa replied, "my mother used to call me Punky as a nick-name, because I looked like Punky Brewster as a kid!" For most girls *Punky Brewster* was a big show in the 80/90's. Nobody would have known this connection. Vanessa said a little something to her Mom before her reading: "Mom, if you're gonna come through, you better make sure I know it's you!" Her Mom also wanted to make sure her daughter knew that, although her life was cut short due to a sudden illness, she's grateful to have had a beautiful bond with her, and that's exactly what she honored most in this lifetime. She was also around Vanessa's boys, and she said the youngest boy sees her, so not to dismiss him. She said she's always going to be around them, loving and guiding them from the other side. A frequent sign will be Cardinals. Vanessa sees cardinals quite often and looks out for these signs and says hello to her mother every day now. They're continuing to work on their spiritual relationship because Love never dies and the soul lives on forever.

Angels are always among us!

CHAPTER TWENTY SEVEN:

Heart-Shaped Cookies with Babcia

Ella was a younger girl who came to me during a very challenging time of her life. Most of my readings are over the phone at this time. I said to her, "Your grandmother's here with us; she's showing me how well you took care of her during the last stages of her life." Ella confirmed her grandmother and her were very close. Her grandmother helped raise her as a child and pour more love into her life, because her mother was emotionally absent at times, and poured more love into her life than she knew what to do with it. Her passing was extremely difficult to navigate, and Ella felt like, how does one beat with half a heart? We must all feel this at some point! Grandma told me that she was from Poland and they called her Babcia. She pointed to her brown locks of hair and then she showed me her small feet and how they had bunions on them that she needed to have repaired. She showed me a thimble and sewing items that she was proud of. Ella confirmed she was a well-known seamstress.

She then started to apologize; she wanted me to apologize to her granddaughter for causing a ruckus getting her to take a shower or brush her teeth. Ella laughed. Oftentimes, her grandmother gave her a really hard time during bath time, as if she were a toddler. She wanted her to remember the good times; they often made pierogies together and, specifically, heart-shaped cookies with fruit jams in the center. She kept showing me a heart-shaped cookie cutter. Ella gasped and said her sister is getting a heart-shaped cookie cutter tattoo in memory of her Babcia! She wanted Ella to tell her sister it was okay that she wasn't there to say goodbye, because she knew she was having much regret after her passing. Her grandmother wanted her to know that, oftentimes, she was taking trips to the other side during her illness with Alzheimer's dementia and that she was greeted by many past loved ones to help her transition. Ella confirmed she often wondered about this—that her grandmother would talk as if other people were there. She wanted me to assure Ella to have no fear for where she is, that she is no longer in pain from her arthritis, that she is free from the burdens of Alzheimer's dementia. Babcia started talking about the rosary and old family pictures from JCPenney. Ella indicated she was holding her rosary right now while on the phone with me, then laughed because they still have pictures of her and her siblings from JCPenney right in the next room. We laughed: who still takes JCPenney pictures, so 90's! Babcia was talking about her rare light blue car she loved and how badly she wants to drive it now, but it was okay they sold it. She understood why they had to take it away from her in her later years due to her diagnosis, and she wanted everyone to know she sends her LOVE from the other side.

Babcia kept saying in Polish, "Kocham cie and dziekuje," which means "I love you, and thank you." Also, I needed to make sure Ella knows how thankful she is for her as her granddaughter in this lifetime and that she has a heart of gold; she'll forever treasure the amount of time and effort she put into her care. Ella badly needed to hear that; she was so lost after her grandmother's passing and told me she felt like she was "on cloud nine" after our session, a session beautiful for both of us.

CHAPTER TWENTY EIGHT:

Block Party!
Flower Bed Ashes

I met Kressa collecting donations one day for our yearly block party. I was so nervous walking up to this construction building, for some reason, but I knew I was led by Spirit, and the task wasn't something I could ignore anymore. Kressa was so excited and gave a generous donation from her construction company. Block parties were something her father threw every year. She told me she was sad, because her dad's death anniversary was coming up, and she really missed him. She felt me coming to her about block parties was a sign. We had an instant connection, so I told her I was a nurse yet also gifted with medium abilities. Later that evening Kressa found me on Facebook and nervously asked me for a reading. Once we started right away her father came through and told me that he passed suddenly from heart and lung trouble. He wanted Kressa to stop beating herself up for trying to prevent the inevitable, and to stop replaying ways to save him. Rather, it may be, she helped him eat better or took him to his doctor's visits. Kressa felt helpless, like she could have stopped her father's death. His time had come to go, he said to me, and he completed his life's path and purposes here on Earth. God called him home. He wanted her and the rest of the family to know he loved them all so very much and that life on the other side is similar to here. He then showed me the number 8; she confirmed that was his birthday. He was big about his birthday! He then showed me the numbers 18 and 24; she said those were the numbers for NASCAR: Jeff Gordon was #24, dad's guy, and Kressa had the m&m car, number 18. They often watched Nascar together at family gatherings. He then said he was still golfing with some of his buddies. She laughed, and found comfort in that.

Kressa's father then said, "Howdie!" Kressa had just bought her grandson a *Toy Story* Andy doll that, when you pull the lever it says, "Howdie partner!" Of course, he wanted her to know he's around his lovable great grandson. Then he started laughing and gave me an elbow nudge and said, "Ask her about the porch." I felt he referenced something very funny; even I couldn't stop laughing. So Kressa said, "Yeah, my dad used to sit by the front porch, so my mom put some of his ashes out in front by the flower beds. Recently, they had to dig up all the flower beds thanks to a collapsed sewer line. The guys took all the dirt away, and all of a sudden my mom remembered his ashes were all in there! So, she had chased down the truck to get them to come back.

Luckily, the guys weren't too far gone, so they stopped, and she made something up and said to the guys, I need the dirt for the back of my house. She didn't want to say, "Oh, my dead husband is in there." We laughed so hard, and then he proceeded to show me birds, like cardinals and blue jays, then, crystal clear, a wood-pecker. Kressa was recently on her yearly girls' trip and saw tons of beautiful birds, but one morning she dealt with an annoying woodpecker right outside their cabin, making so much noise it would wake them up! I said, "that's your dad for ya!" Kressa and I became close friends with all of this spirituality. Kressa sent me so many of her soul sisters that are either intuitive themselves or open to this kind of spirituality; I feel like they're all beautiful puzzle pieces to this group. We definitely have a great connection, and I know her father placed me in her path!

"The soul is invisible. An angel is invisible.
The wind is invisible. Thoughts are invisible.
And yet, with sensitivity, you can see the soul,
you can guess the angel, you can feel the wind,
you can change the world with only a few thoughts."
– Paulo Coelho

CHAPTER TWENTY NINE:

My Father the Hero and a Mother's Everlasting Love

Sammy, who is now in her mid 50's, lost her mother at the tender age of six. Her mother was pregnant with her baby sister when she found out she had breast cancer, and her father raised her up until she was fifteen years old, at which time he lost his life to cancer. Her father had to make the utmost difficult decision to have a couple from church adopt her baby sister in case he, too, wouldn't survive cancer. Sometimes, while Sammy's father was too sick and in and out of the hospital, this couple would help out and take care of Sammy as well. They fell in love with Sammy's baby sister and adopted her prior to her father's death. Sammy was alone, and then went to live with her 21-year-old brother, as they were both pretty much left out in this world to manage on their own. Sammy ended up marrying the love of her life at nineteen years old and is still with him, but she always had this void throughout her life from the loss of her parents. Sammy came to me in hopes to connect with her loving parents from the other side. That morning of the reading, my step dad was with me in spirit, and very strongly, too. I understand he's my guide now, but he was more connected to my energy than usual, as if he had a surprise.

Once the reading started, Sammy's father came through with my step dad in uniform; they were laughing. It turns out they worked together at the same police department. My step dad was at the beginning of his career and helped take over Sammy's father's position back in 1972. Sammy's father was leaving to work as a sergeant at the local college police department, a job within walking distance of his house. What a small world! Sammy doesn't even live in this area anymore. Her father wanted her to know that he was with his brother on the other side, her

uncle Bob. Along with Uncle Bob came his white little poodle
Buffy. They were so happy and free. Sammy's dad kept talking
about how proud he was of her, that she finally got her driver's
license! After her father's death, she was anxious about driving (I
can relate) and didn't have her father there to teach her, since he
had just passed from cancer. He was calm and gentle and understanding. Her father was her hero in this life, and not just for
her, but for many others, serving, as he did, as a police officer.

Sammy had a really grumpy Driver's Ed teacher who would
scold her and slam on the brakes and belittle her. During that
difficult time of her life, she just gave up on driving. Again, I
could totally relate to her story. It wasn't until Sammy was in her
30's that she finally had the courage to get her driver's license
so that she could take her kids to places. Her father came in so
proud of her and wanted her to know she will always be Daddy's
little girl. Also, she needed to make sure she had jumper cables
with her at all times. Sammy didn't understand why, but later,
after our reading, her car died; luckily she was in her driveway;
it needed to be jumped. Her Dad then showed me the numbers
13 and 23; he kept referencing January. Turns out, her Dad's
birthday was the 13th, and her son's birthday is the 23rd, both
in January. Although he wasn't here when her son was born,
during such a big time in her life, he wanted her to know he is
loving and guiding her son from the other side and happy about
what a beautiful mother she has become.

Sammy's Mom stepped forward and wanted her to know she is
so happy with the beautiful wife and mother, sister and woman

she became. She wanted her to know she knows she still has her favorite gold bracelet. Sammy confirmed this. Her mother was flawless and beautiful, comparable to Marilyn Monroe. Sammy's mom wanted her to know the dream was real and that she was with her during another most difficult time of her life, and helped save her. Sammy had dreamt of her mother prior to her surgery for breast cancer. She had a double mastectomy. Her mother wasn't sick anymore. In the dream, she was healthy and as beautiful as ever, and gave her a big hug; the dream felt so real. Sammy's breast cancer was caught early due to her mother's diagnosis. Sammy always felt like her mother had something to do with the healing stages of her illness.

Sammy felt abandoned and lost most of her life without her parents, a tough time and huge transition for her. Her mother had just given birth, and then her father had to give her baby sister up for adoption, because he had just gotten his own cancer diagnosis. He wanted to make sure the baby went to a good family. Deep down in his soul, he knew he wasn't going to make it. After Sammy's reading, she felt closure, and everything that she thought she knew and second- guessed was true, that her family was always close to her, helping her from the other side.

> *"Closure. We all seek it. We seek the end of things but also the beginning of new things."*
> *– Unknown*

CHAPTER THIRTY:

The Crown of a Woman is Her Hair!

I was getting my hair done, enjoying some self-care mommy me time, and Spirit kept trying to come through. We were deep in conversation. I told my hair stylist I'm a medium, and she was genuinely intrigued. "I see a tall man standing there next to you; he said his name is Pete." She immediately had chills run throughout her body: Pete was her grandfather's name. He kept showing me a turtle garden stone, and she said he really loved his garden. He also told me that his real name wasn't Pete, but a longer Italian name. He shortened it, so people could pronounce it easier. Don't worry, Pete, I know the feeling! My stylist confirmed this. He was sending his love from the other side and brought with him his wife. A much shorter woman was standing next to him, pointing excitedly to her curly brown hair; she wanted her granddaughter to know she had her hair back!

My hair stylist's grandmother passed away early in life due to a brain tumor. After operations and chemotherapy, she lost her beautiful brown curly hair. She was always specific about her hair! She considered her hair the crown of her beauty and she always had it well kept. She then kept repeating the name Maria; my stylist confirmed that was her grandmother's name. She showed me a stocking full of candy she would get for her granddaughter; she hoped she could remember all of the good times that they had; then she was holding a cat. My hairstylist had just recently lost her beloved cat of many years.

They want her to know the expert way she fixes women's "crowns" (hair) is her soul's life path and purpose. She should continue to provide that type of "healing" to women everywhere. They also wanted their granddaughter to know they were always around her—and that they will help her make big decisions coming up within her life and relationships. Lastly, they wished to let her mother know they were with her during this difficult time. My hairstylist said her mother had just taken a bad fall and was going through a difficult time with the pain. She loved communicating with her beloved grandparents; sometimes she feels lost without them, and lost on this path of life. I just loved how they chose this moment of beauty shop to get a quick message to their loving granddaughter.

CHAPTER THIRTY ONE:

Walking with Jesus, Bunny Rabbits, Wheel of Fortune, Cheesecake in Heaven, OH, MY!

Leah Rae came to me because she wanted to connect with her dad. She missed him terribly; he had just recently passed, but the first person who came through was her beloved friend who was more like a sister, named Barbara Allen. They were very close spiritually, and Barbara Allen helped Leah Rae with many aspects of life. If not for Barbara Allen, Leah Rae wouldn't have known much about the spiritual world. Barbara Allen was into hypnosis, yoga, and meditation, all very important, and past life regression; she was a gifted medium, as well. Like me, Barbara Allen had a bad childhood and turned her horrific events into love and light. Consequently, I was not surprised she stepped forward with Leah Rae's son. I believe in the importance of having an adult bring through a child from the other side. Her son, Luca, passed away at just about seven months old back in 1993, from an ear infection that turned into bacterial meningitis. His death created a huge domino effect on their family and the community.

When we get knocked down, we tend to look for the light and open up spiritually, and for Leah Rae that was just the case. Leah Rae went through a deep amount of grief, because how can one explain the numbness of losing a child? As a grieving mother, Leah Rae was in shock for a long time and probably shouldn't have gotten pregnant with her daughter right away, but she just had a loss of identity; she was still Luca's mother: she didn't know what to do with herself anymore. She felt like she was in a dream barely existing in this world. Over time, during her spiritual awakening, she wrote a letter to Luca's doctor, consoling him about the loss of Luca. Luca's doctor dismissed his ear

infection and gave medications, confident he would be fine. The
doctor felt horrible when Luca's illness took a turn for the worse.
His doctor saved that letter and carried it with him to work; he
even helped push the meningitis vaccine for children after the
passing of Luca. Leah Rae ended up holding in so much regret
for her son's passing, blaming herself for his death. Leah Rae
started to notice toys and lights and tvs going on and off: Luca
even would make his spirit known when people came to visit the
house. The lights would flicker; the family got to the point of
saying, "Hey, Luca! We know you're here!"

During our reading, Luca wanted his mommy to know that,
although his life was cut short, he signed up for it in a sense: he
just wanted to be loved beyond measure. And he sure was! He
chose Leah Rae and his dad to be his parents in this lifetime, so
he could provide a quick few lessons to those here on Earth. He
also said to me, "Tell my mommy to stop blaming herself and
to be set free from that guilt bottling up inside after all these
years." He then said, "Tell my mommy I am walking with Jesus
and that I am a very evolved soul up there with the messengers."
Leah Rae cried. She has his pictures set up next to a little statue
of Jesus walking with a boy. That message was beyond validating.

Leah Rae often wondered what Luca's first moments of walking
would have been like. He was only seven months old before he
passed. Luca was a very evolved soul; his short life was all part
of his soul's path and purpose; he is still loved and still loves
and guides his parents and family from the other side. He let
me know his mommy's birthday, which is on the 9th, further

to validate his spirit with us. Leah Rae cried during our session; she wasn't expecting her son to come through twenty-seven years after his passing. She needed this closure; she needed to heal after all that time since her beloved son's life on earth had ended.

Next, Leah Rae's father-in-law stepped forward in uniform to validate his time in the Korean War and how proud he was to serve his country during those times. He also desired to let her know "life" was amazing on the other side; he was so happy he was able to do a visitation like this. In life he was very religious and did not believe in mediums. He literally went to church when here on Earth. He wanted to apologize for being so judgmental and letting his religious views hold him back in some ways, but he was here to pass a message along and let Leah Rae know he was watching over them. He indicated he was also with his friend Henry, who was sick with a severe infection at the time; he was going to help provide healing to him. Henry was set to have his leg removed, but ended up fully recovering shortly after our session. Her father-in-law wanted her to know cheesecake exists in heaven, and he was once again enjoying all of his sweets!

Finally, Leah Rae's father stepped forward. He wanted her to know he constantly visited her in her dreams, which she confirmed. He was laughing and walking again and able to shower himself now. He kept showing me his once swollen leg and feet. Now he had no more swelling and leg pain! He desired to thank Leah Rae for helping to care for him and confirmed one of his last life lessons was to learn to be taken care of in this life. Throughout his entire lifetime, he had been the one to take care of everybody else. He also said he was still sitting in his favorite chair, watching the game show *Wheel Of Fortune* every night. Then he showed me his little lap dog in spirit with him, a Chihuahua sitting on his lap, and a bunny rabbit as well. (Yes, animals cross over and have souls too). He wanted to make sure his family knew he had his beloved Chihuahua on his lap, as usual.

Leah Rae let her mom know about what came through in the reading, and she was shocked; she said she still watches *Wheel Of Fortune* every night and puts his bunny rabbit in his favorite chair: the bunny rabbit she bought him from the gift shop while he was in the hospital. He would get really nervous, so she wanted him to have something to hold. Leah Rae was so shocked her mom still had the bunny rabbit. She was amazed her father provided such detail to me. Shortly after our session, Leah Rae found a card from her soul sister friend Barbara Allen. It read, "Here on Earth and the other side, I will always be with you!" Leah Rae has reached out to me after finding it; I knew it made her heart happy. She felt so healed after our session.

CHAPTER THIRTY TWO:

Gym Shoes

I grew up with Emma Berry. She had been really good friends with my brother Antonio since elementary school, and we would keep in touch here and there over the years. We would joke and laugh and talk about the good old days. Word got around about my readings, and so she reached out with the need to connect with her beloved brother. I didn't know Emma's brother; he was a bit older than us, so we didn't go to school together. Emma, like many, had fallen into a deep depression after the loss of her brother. When I read Emma, immediately, her brother came through before I could even get on the phone with her. I said to him, "You better give me something I have no clue about, so she doesn't think I'm pulling this out of my ass." He kept talking about his gym shoes, and I'm like, "Okay, are these some expensive gym shoes like Jordans, or what?" He was like, "You will see…"

When we got on the phone to start the reading, I said to Emma, "Listen, your brother is here, and he says you have his gym shoes!" She laughed and said, "Yep, I saved his gym shoes!" I replied, "What! Are they really nice Jordans or something you can pass down to your teenage son?" She replied, "Nope they're old and dirty and really worn out, and it was just something that I felt I needed to save from his belongings." We both laughed, because they were so ugly and full of mud! She just couldn't part with her brother's gym shoes! He wanted her to know that he was with their grandma and many others on the other side, and he now, of course, was cancer free. He then proceeded to thank her for doing everything she could to help him during his battle with brain cancer and for desperately trying to save him. But, now it was her time to take care of herself, mentally, physically, and, most importantly, spiritually. Tell her, "Now is the time to stop messing around," he said, "and get on your true life's path and purpose." Emma, too, was a gifted healer, but her intuition was causing her too much anxiety, and she was frequently self-medicating to help ease the pain from grief—as well as the anxiety caused by the spirit world she tried to shut out. So, Emma, of course, shed a few tears of healing during our session. Since then she has listened and is on the path of healing herself and learning about the gifts and abilities she has. Emma set up a healing session with Pat Longo and is now working on herself the way her brother requested she do.

Your Angels are with you right now.

CHAPTER THIRTY THREE:

Auntie Gracie
Our Family's
Sweetheart

Christmas time will forever and always be the most memorable times with our Auntie Gracie. She always hosted Christmas for everyone, and she was always dressed in her lovely Christmas sweaters with her dangling Christmas earrings. She provided some brief magic for us kids growing up. The tree was real, and it was huge, and if she could afford something for everyone, she put those items underneath the tree. I remember getting a Barbie doll under that big pine Christmas tree one year, and I felt so loved. Every year I received Christmas cards from her; they were always so beautifully written. She was so sweet, just like the special Auntie one could see in movies. Auntie Gracie was married to my grandma's brother. My Grandma Honey always said her brother sure lucked out with the wife God gave him. Auntie Gracie was just heavenly, our earth angel—not a mean bone in her body. Her voice was so soft and sweet, and she was so kind; she always saw the good in everyone. I'm convinced she was a secret earth angel, so when God called her home that day, I wasn't surprised He needed our angel back. Auntie Gracie went to Heaven on the same day my step dad did, but a year later. Our family once again was devastated and wondered why God continued to take the good ones. Auntie Gracie developed an infection, and it spread to her blood, until she went septic. Her body and organs completely shut down.

I was so grateful to say my last "I love you" and goodbye to my Auntie Gracie. Her daughter put the phone by Gracie's ear in the hospital bed. After her passing, I told her when she is ready she can come to me in a dream, and she did! I walked into a lunchroom, and I saw her, full-figured and healthy again. She was the Lunch Lady! She would make sure all of the children were fed and well cared for. Let me tell you, the food looked amazing and freshly made. Not just sloppy joes like kids regularly get these days! I saw blueberry crepes and fresh fruits and vegetables, all laid out beautifully. I felt like I had traveled back in time, and I was so happy to experience her spirit once again. I let one of her daughter's know about my dream, and I said she was the Lunch Lady. She was so happy to hear that and asked how she looked. I said she was happy, healthy, and full-figured again. My cousin said to me, when she and her sisters were little girls, Auntie Gracie was the Lunch Lady at their school. It was something I never knew about her. I was thrilled she came to me with something so validating that only her loving daughters knew about. Once again, I felt privileged to be the messenger from the other side. Her daughters just wanted to know she was alright. I felt Auntie Gracie chose to reenact that time of her life because that was a time she was loved the most. She loved when her three girls were so innocent and little. She loved being able to work at their school as the Lunch Lady and provide love and food to all the children of the community, just like she had done throughout her entire lifetime. That dream, or what we all know was a visit from Heaven, remains a beautiful message to share with all of you.

Life sure isn't the same without our sweet Auntie Gracie. Her daughters and my uncle struggle daily since her passing. One of her daughter's had her first birthday without her mom. While she was opening birthday cards at the dinner table, out of nowhere, a feather was on the place mat next to her. She knew her mom was with her at that moment, hoping to let her know she is with her in spirit. She called her sister who was driving home at the time and who had just bought her first home in many years since her divorce. She told her to be on the lookout for feathers as a sign from mom. Once she arrived at home, she found a feather on her front porch! Auntie Gracie wanted her to know how happy she was about her new home and that she will be there with her. Don't worry if on earth you move places; spirit can find you! Heaven has its own address book. Our family was now on the lookout for signs from our sweet Auntie Gracie.

My mom stopped by one day; I told her how her cousins were getting all these feathers from their mother. We were all talking about it. The doorways to Heaven were wide open thanks to everyone talking about these beautiful signs. My mom soon left to go to the grocery store; she was sitting in the parking lot, making sure she had everything. When she pulled out her wallet, out popped this big beautiful white fluffy feather. My mom thought someone was messing with her, because we literally were just talking about signs from Heaven. She was trying to make sense of the incident and wrap her head around it. She called me to ask, "Did you put a feather in my purse?" I laughed and said, "No, mom, but that's how these signs from Heaven work! Auntie Gracie sends her love to you, too, now. Why shouldn't she? She loved us all so much, and she wanted us all to know she was, and is, still around us all in her spirit form."

Love is limitless; it never dies. Signs from your loved ones in Heaven are just another way to show everlasting love to their loved ones that are still here on earth. Be open to the signs; continue to talk about them with your loved ones. You'll be surprised what shows up! We are never so lost that our Angels cannot find us!

CHAPTER THIRTY FOUR:

Jack and His Pennies

Jack regularly handed out graham crackers to most of the young kids on his block, and every Halloween, he would put out cases of pop for the trick or treaters. He had a love for game shows and was addicted to watching the Lifetime movies all day long. I swear he could watch the movies on mute and still know them word for word. Jack had endless boxes of items delivered from the QVC Channel, and oftentimes, it was a thoughtful gift for someone else. We had a loving relationship; I was his primary caretaker and nurse for the last year of his life, so we grew quite close to one another. We would joke a lot, but he could also be profound. He quoted something to me that stuck: "If you can't show love, don't show hate." In other words, either be loving or be playful in your attacks; never act out of hate.

As I continued to care for Jack I was always with him and his wife during the week and weekends, even on the holidays, to make sure they were properly cared for. We talked about life and past regrets, and even death. He said to me, "When I die, toss my ashes to the wind. C'est la vie!" He told me how he felt helpless during his early years of fatherhood when he had a drinking problem, but when he went to rehab, he really enjoyed helping all the others while there. I believe he was a true empath. On Sunday mornings, when Mass was on the local channel, he would ask me to sit with him to watch it together and to pray. I told him about my spiritual gifts, and he laughed and said that would spook him out to have such a gift. When he needed to go to the hospital, I begged him to go: he was just that stubborn. I didn't want his only daughter to find him on the floor one day; he was having major heart and breathing issues. He finally gave in and went. By then he had multiple health issues. He asked his nurse for an anxiety pill in the middle of the night, and after she gave him one, he said, "Alright, thank you, I'm ready to go home." The nurse looked at him confused because the doctor never gave him an order for discharge, especially not for 1 a.m.. Shortly after, the nurse came in to check on him and he had passed away peacefully in his sleep. A soul knows when it is time. I feel when all the energy of their angels and passed loved ones comes to get them, they get so anxious.

After his passing, I began to find pennies in odd places: on my driveway, on my window sill, and even on the floor in my bathroom. I told Jack, "Thank you for the signs," but laughed and said to him, "can you step it up a notch?" (One hundred dollar bills would have been nice!) I still continued to take care of his elderly wife who had dementia, and that's when the phones would continue to ring and ring in her room with nobody on the other line. The caller ID just showed the numbers 111 or 555 or 777, all within sequence—as if Heaven were calling. I knew that was Jack calling, showing us he was okay in Heaven, that his transition was made smoothly—but the phone calls wouldn't stop. At some point his young grandson, Jack Jr., picked up the phone and said, "I know it's you, grandpa, and I know you're okay, but you can stop calling now." Sure enough, the phone calls stopped! I was laughing inside because I told Jack to step it up, and he sure did. I still find pennies to this day; I tell him thank you; he knows how much I truly miss him and his wife. He even came to me in a dream once to let me know he was so happy and didn't need any more medications. "Life is surely grand in Heaven; thank you for our time together."

"We are all just walking each other home."
– Ram Daas

CHAPTER THIRTY FIVE:

Little Leprechaun

My rival sister asked me to do a reading for her: ya know, one of the ones who would chalk me up as being crazy, ready to brand me a nutso, yet who might have similar gifts as myself. I keep telling my siblings they're not sick, they're psychic!

Well, with all of the positive feedback she heard about me in the neighborhood, she got curious enough to ask me for a reading. I gave in and agreed to read her. I thought reading someone in my Soul Group might be hard because we are already connected in certain ways, but boy, was I wrong. Right away I saw a young guy in his teens. I thought to myself, "there's no way this is for my sister; this must be for her boyfriend, right?" I kept going back and forth with myself. I said to her, "I see a young guy here; he's skinny and small, and he says he lived through a rough upbringing, and he passed suddenly from a motorcycle accident. Do you know him?" I thought I knew everyone she knows who has passed.

Right away she said, "Yes I do! I had a really good friend I never brought around to you guys back in the day because he hung out with the wrong crowd. He was in an accident; his family couldn't afford to bury him, so he was cremated." In a bit of shock, I proceeded; I said, "he's talking about how you guys would hang out and smoke pot in the garages together like most teenagers and how he was really a 'Dennis the Menace.' He's showing me the skate park where he would often go and has his shirt off standing in front of me with his skateboard." My rival sister yelled, "Yes, yes, yes." Next he laughed with us and showed me his scabbed elbow, and my sister was like, "Oh my god! He had this scabbed elbow, and he would just continue to pick at it and peel it off in front of me to gross me out!" We laughed.

To continue I indicated we were now headed to the local Pool, where we "lived" every summer and called ma collect from the pay phones to bring us food or pick us up to go home. I said, "It's night...I'm standing in front of the very big white fences. I feel as though we are about to hop the fence and go skinny dipping in the pool!" She laughed and said, "Not skinny dipping, but we all snuck in at night and started going down the water slides together!" I wondered why me and my friends never did this together. I always wanted to sneak into the pools in the summertime, but never did! Then I said to her, "Your friend is getting really comfortable now, and since he and I are friends, or so he thinks, he finds it funny to just whip out his 'banana': he's flashing me." By now my sister laughed harder through her tears; that's exactly what her friend would do to them. He was impulsive and would just do random things like that!

My sister's friend then showed me all of his tattoos, especially the little leprechaun Fighting Irish Guy; she said "Oh my God! That's exactly what we would call him". Her friend was probably only fourteen at the time, and his dad allowed him to get a tattoo. He was short and always shirtless, and we would call him "The Little Leprechaun" because he had red hair! I said, "he wants you to tell his brothers he's with them and that he messes with his dad while he drinks beer in the garage. He knows his mother is in a dark space and has never been the same since his passing. He is with her, too."

He was such a good friend and was so funny, so he and my sister bonded through their humor and rough upbringing. He really wanted my sister to know that although fifteen earth years have gone by since his passing, he was truly around her still to this day, very much the same Little Leprechaun inside of Heaven. Although his life was cut short and fast lived; he wasn't here for a long time but a good time. His short life was a lesson to the rest of their group to shape up and stay in school away from and off drugs.

My sister was amazed and in awe; those times were far away; some from that group of friends had lost touch; they continued down the wrong path. My sister, too, like many of my siblings, shares similar gifts as me, and now, instead of self-medicating away the pain, she has started the path of healing all of our childhood traumas, so she can expand her gifts and abilities. She shocked herself with the accurate readings of healing messages now she provides to people, and all I have to say is, "I told ya so!" The "crazier", more anxious you are, my friends, the more likely you are to share these gifts!

> *"And those who were seen dancing were thought to be insane by those who could not hear the music."*
> *– Friedrich Nietzsche*

CHAPTER THIRTY SIX:

Forever a Mama's Boy

Jenny came to me last year in hopes of connecting with the other side since the loss of her beloved three-year-old son Nico, to a rare seizure disorder. Jenny was lost and fragile when speaking to me. Right away, her son came in bouncing, like a ball full of energy! He was standing in his Batman costume with his Spidey undies. He wanted his mommy to know he chose her and his father because they were able to provide so much fierce love for him in such a short time, fierce love most people long for throughout a lifetime. He said, "I chose them knowing they would continue to fight for me and raise awareness about this rare seizure disorder." They traveled all over to various doctors and even to Boston's Children's Hospital for critical research regarding his medical needs. "Please, let my mommy know I am aware of all the nice things everyone has done in my honor: the memory blankets and teddy bears, and the balloon releases." He even brought up the garden stone his mommy wanted to have made for him with his adorable little face on it. He talked about how Jenny still has all of his belongings and how she cannot part with any of them; he confirmed she should hold on to them for as long as she needs or wants.

Most importantly, he talked about the handprints the hospital gave her prior to his passing. He desperately wants his mommy to know that, at the end of his life here on Earth, he was hooked up to so many machines, and despite his parents' fight, eager to never give up on him, his tiny little body shut down, and he was already on the other side. His mommy had some powerful decisions to make; he is forever grateful she made the right decision letting him go. I said, "He's with your loving father and not alone; he's actually a more evolved soul than you and I, Jenny. He wants to validate the toys going off and the lights flickering in his room to try to get your attention. He wants you to know that he is always and forever a Mama's Boy, and that, although it's hard for you to know, Jenny, deep down, your soul knows this was part of the plan. He chose his cute little face and this short-lived contract on Earth to gain spiritual awareness and medical awareness for his medical issues, so that, in the long run, he can save others just like him." He then showed me the numbers 7 19, and that was in reference to something important coming up. Jenny started to cry and said she was going on that date to her fertility doctor to transfer embryos in hopes for another baby.

Jenny is now pregnant with a little girl, and she is going to name her Honor in honor of Nico. Jenny is a Medium, herself, and her personal experiences have helped her to open up to her gifts.

CHAPTER THIRTY SEVEN:

Free Bird

Francesca came to me to connect with the other side in hopes that her younger cousin Joey would come through. She needed closure because she couldn't wrap her mind around the fact that his young vibrant self was no longer with them. Joey had a very loving, close family; in fact they were so close they lived next door to their grandparents as well. They even built a fence with a door that leads to their backyard, where they had many gatherings.

When our session started Francesca's Grandpa came through standing there in his plaid shirt, one he normally wore. He wanted her to know that he was with her during her most difficult time of divorcing her abusive husband. He wanted her to know he was guiding her through it. He was so happy about where she was in her present point of life; he of course, also wished to remind her of how beautiful she is. He then showed me his wallet and the beautiful picture he still kept of her as a girl. Francesca cried with tears of joy because after his death, she found the wallet with her high school picture still in there from over a decade ago! He also told me to tell Francesca to knock off the smoking, that it was not good for her! "Make sure you get your car serviced soon too!" Francesca laughed and said, "Yeah, it was about time for an oil change; my grandpa usually reminded me about such things."

He showed me he had her beloved cat Smokey with him on the other side and that he was taking good care of him. Also, he indicated that the dream she had was a true visitation from him. He wanted her to let Nonni (grandma) know he was sorry for being so grumpy, and to tell the family "Hello" from the other side: he was doing alright and still in his favorite places. "Make sure they bring my favorite pudding pie to the family gathering for Thanksgiving coming up!" Francesca laughed and said he loved that specific pie!

Then a younger male stepped forward but his energy was a bit gray, a bit weaker than most souls coming through. He stood behind the grandpa and came out when it was his time. I felt grandpa had to help push him through a bit, but when he started to show me things there was no turning back! I will say his passing on earth was self-inflicted, and he was taking responsibility for his departure. Francesca agreed and indicated this was definitely cousin Joey whom she had been waiting to hear from. Joey right away showed me a tree and some big writing on it. Francesca cried yet could take all of this. Her cousin Joey committed suicide by slamming his car at full speed right into a tree. After his passing, Joey's family and friends gathered around the tree to build a memorial and put his initials on the tree, very big for everyone to see and remember him. They even wrote his initials on the tree in their families' joint backyard.

Joey wanted Francesca to tell the family it was in those last moments he wanted to take back his impulsive decision to end his life. He was so sorry for the hardship and sadness he caused the family. He wanted his mother to know that he knows she is in a dark place herself ever since his passing, and that he hears her when she talks to him. He knows her dream was to find comfort knowing he is in a better place despite his self inflicted death. He wanted her to start living again. He needs her to realize it's not her time to go be with him. She needs to stay. "Please let her know that!" He wanted her to know he messes with the lights. Francesca said that her aunt put up the Christmas tree early this year and sometimes the lights on the tree would switch on and off when nobody touched them. He knows her Aunt is also severely depressed and no longer wants to live her life.

Joey wanted to let his brother know that it was him he saw standing in the hallway, "so no, you're not going crazy." Francesca was shocked because Joey's brother had thought he was indeed going crazy after he saw his brother standing there—convinced it was just deep grief messing with his imagination.

He wants everyone to continue to remember him as the shirtless, handsome guy with a six pack. The family should no longer fall into the traps of the "what if, should have, could have, would have game" surrounding his passing. He wanted everyone to stop replaying the possibility of saving him. He was taking full responsibility for his actions. He now sees how much Love and support he had throughout his community, family, and friends. He now knows he could have and should have chosen a different route by healing himself through therapy and the help of mental health care professionals. "Everything was available to me, BUT I was a prisoner in my own mind and I suffered daily with depression. This was chemical! This was very serious and I knew I needed help, but I made a plan that day to end my life and for that I'm sorry."

Joey then brought forward a girl from the block they grew up with. He wanted Francesca to know they were playing "Ghost in the Graveyard" and all the old school night time games they used to play in the summertime. Francesca was wiping her tears away and said there was a girl they grew up with who passed suddenly from an illness. Joey wanted everyone to know he was not alone. He wanted the family to know he was like "a caged bird set free." His soul was no longer in a dark place, and although he suffered from depression, in that split moment it was his mental illness that controlled him. Please tell them to allow themselves to heal and celebrate my life with more backyard celebrations. He will continue to send signs to his loved ones, who must trust he is not in a dark place on the other side. He's with grandpa and the girl down the block. They'll guide him and help his soul evolve and grow on the other side. He too was Inside of Heaven just like the others.

"Suicide doesn't end the chances of life getting worse; it eliminates the possibility of it never getting any better."
– Unknown

Do not hesitate to call the National Suicide Prevention Lifeline, 1-800-273-8255.

CHAPTER THIRTY EIGHT:

Grandma Honey

My mom says one way she would describe her mother was that she was so driven to get things done. She didn't put up with anyone, especially any man's crap; nevertheless, she did give others a chance to prove themselves. She was always there for her two daughters and us grandkids. She was hilarious, like Betty White. She had unique things and cool cars, like a maroon Camaro and a vintage Chicago Bulls jacket. She really just loved life. She was always calling you, "Sweetie or Honey," and that's why my kids gave her the nickname Grandma Honey. She was always happy or cracking jokes; even though tough events happened, she kept a smile on her face, so that none of us kids knew something was wrong. She was definitely a woman to be seen on the dance floor!

My Grandma Honey was just different; she wasn't the typical granny. She always had her purse by her side and would yell at you if you left yours open! She was the one granny who stood out and all of our friends loved! When we threw house parties growing up, she handed out solo cups for $5 dollars while you stood in line for the keg. Grandma Honey would hide her Little Debbie oatmeal cakes, and her bags of Kit Kat bars, but she always made us a bagel with tea and honey or a Chicago style hot dog with half of a pickle. She was the greatest Love for us all.

My grandma had COPD and a weakening heart, so when the end of her life here on Earth neared, I, being the nurse of the family, was able to care for her. I knew she was getting ready to make her transition soon because at night I could hear her from the baby monitor talking to the Angels in her sleep. She also started to let go of things and asked me if I wanted some of her shoes, because she wasn't going to be needing them any longer. I was so grateful to be able to do something for her, since she was always taking care of us growing up as kids and even into our adult years. I was able to help her with her meals and tuck her into bed at night and kiss her on the forehead. I was able to help her with the tasks she just didn't want to do anymore or was afraid to do. I fed her, dressed her, and bathed her.

Oftentimes, she would argue with me about helping her into the shower, and one time she sat naked on the toilet seat, just looking at her body in awe of what was happening to it, asking herself and God why this was happening to her. I said, "Don't worry, Gramma Honey, look, my body has changed, too!" and I flashed her my boobs; she was like, "Oh my god; put those things away! What's the matter with you, wear a bra, you've got boobs like an old lady!" We just laughed and laughed!

All of that laughter and care I was able to provide was such an honor for me; I always consider taking care of the elderly with the utmost love and respect they deserve, to be a high honor. While helping her into bed one night, Grandma Honey said to me that the best way to go would be in one's sleep; she hoped that is how she would go. I told her, "I'll make sure to ask God and the angels for that wish." Once her COPD and heart got worse, she ended up in the hospital. When my mom was leaving, that last night, my grandma said to her, "Make sure you take my purse." My mom thought that simple request was a bit odd because she always kept her purse within sight, but we both knew she knew the angels were coming for her. We said our goodbyes, and she said to me, "Make sure you send my Love to the kids."

The next morning, when my mom went to visit her at the hospital, she was still in a sleep-like state and eventually passed later that evening. My mom was so upset with the nurse; she didn't understand why her mom declined so much. The nurse indicated her duty was to make them comfortable, and that my grandma asked just to sleep. I felt that my grandma was so nervous and desperate to transition to the other side without being in pain and suffering. She asked the nurse in the middle of the night for a sleeping pill, so the nurse gave her one. She never took those. I believe that was my grandma's way of trying to control the situation one last time here on Earth: securing the way she wanted to depart from this life to the next. Grandma Honey went peacefully in her sleep, surrounded by loved ones.

Shortly after her arrival to the dance floors of Heaven, Grandma Honey came to me in a dream. I walked into the kitchen by my mom's house, and I saw my step dad John; he said, "Look who I got!" With him was my grandma with a little girl smirk on her face just sitting at the kitchen table, laughing a little bit as if she were in trouble. She knew what she was doing by asking for that sleeping pill; she knew she caused an uproar with the nurse's station and my family. I laughed and shook my head, but I knew she was comfortable, and I know she went peacefully. Every time she comes to me, she's got her big waves of hair flowing in the wind while she's driving her Camaro. She yelled out to me one time, "There's nothing to fear up here! There's nothing to be afraid of!" I used to be in so much fear, and my grandma would always ask me what was the matter. Now that I'm on this path, I feel less egoistic and more free from fear. Fear doesn't stop death; it stops you from truly living.

When I think of my Grandma and miss her, she shows me white butterflies around me and my children. My kids talk to Grandma Honey as if she is right next to them, and I know she is. I will always miss calling her on the phone and singing *Somewhere Over the Rainbow*. If she were busy at the local Jewel or library, I'd sing it to her answering machine the same way Judy Garland sang it, all vintage like. I'd end the voicemail with, "Call me back, ya hussie!" And, we would just laugh and laugh. I hear that song now and I get choked up because it brings me back to those moments. I find peace now that I know she's "Somewhere Over The Rainbow."

Naturally my mom was so sad that my grandma's one year was coming up from when she departed. She wasn't getting any signs from her, until one day she was wrapping Christmas presents in the spare bedroom my Grandma stayed in. All of a sudden she heard her name clear as day from the "frunchroom"— a Chicago term for front room aka living room. She got up and ran so fast to look for her because that's where my grandma sat on the couch and would watch her game shows and yell for my ma to get her attention. My mom called me and said, "I was so desperately convinced it was her and her voice was so clear that I stopped wrapping presents and ran to look for her." I said, "Ma, why wouldn't she call you and send her love; just because you're not getting any visits in dreams or daily signs doesn't mean Grandma Honey ain't around."

Even my sister's dog, my Grandma Honey adored, barks at the chair and gets spooked as if she still sits there when she visits. The tv's and lights flicker. When my sister asked for a sign she so desperately needed, Grandma Honey sure did deliver. My sister wanted to know if her surgery for her hysterectomy would go well, and she hoped to know if the surrogacy would take.

My sister went to the store shortly after her demands for signs, and the cashier's name was Evelyn. When she got home she received a birth announcement from a coworker of a baby girl being born, named Evelyn. That was Grandma Honey's real name!

"I know you're dancin' and singing in the angels' choir"

Sometimes, Grandma Honey's Wizard of Oz music box will start playing "Somewhere Over the Rainbow." That song has so much significance to our family. I'm so grateful to have had the grandmother I did in this life. She was filled with so much love and humor. I think because of her we all share so much love and humor with the world. I'll miss calling her and singing to her answering machine, but I know in my heart of hearts we will all be together once again. I know she's right here next to me when I need her most. I find comfort knowing that Grandma Honey is free of pain and most likely spending a lot of her time at the slot machines or on the dance floors of Heaven with all of our other loved ones. "I love you so much Grandma Honey! With love forever and always, your favorite granddaughter, April. Yes I said it: FAVORITE granddaughter that showered you…... with song and love!"

"A Heart is not judged by how much you love;
but by how much you are loved by others."
– The Wonderful Wizard of OZ

CHAPTER THIRTY NINE:

I Want to Be Inside Your Heaven

Now that I've told you much of my life story, I'm hoping you'll understand Heaven is not up there; it's right here. Heaven is often described as the "highest place," the holiest place, a paradise. I've insisted it's not up there in the sky where we assume Heaven is. Heaven is interdimensional; it's right here and within us. Why wouldn't our loved ones choose us to be their paradise, their infinity, their sweet everlasting Heaven? Their souls, their conscious selves, live on in the afterlife, and they pretty much hang around their Soul Groups yet also take on other jobs while we're here continuing our own soul's contract.

Sometimes people say Heaven on Earth involves helping the elderly or listening to a baby's laugh, or helping the homeless. I truly believe that when we do these things, we follow the Angel's voices.

I want you to know that, when you experience moments of grief, you, in a sense, wonder what the inside of Heaven is like and what your loved ones are up to, or if they're still in pain or suffering. They are right next to you—just a thought away, in their spirit form. Sometimes, they come here for a short time though still evolving on the other side, or sometimes, they live long full lives and are already fully evolved after learning a ton of life lessons and transitioning beautifully. No matter how long they lived, no matter how evolved here on Earth they became, after they get to Heaven, they show us multiple ways to connect with them. To help that along, we can practice journaling, prayer, meditation and paying attention to the signs they send us along the way.

A Jewish Prayer

In the rising of the sun and in its going down, we remember them.

In the glowing of the wind and in the chill of winter, we remember them.

In the opening of buds and in the rebirth of spring, we remember them.

In the blueness of sky and in the warmth of summer, we remember them.

In the rustling of leaves and in the beauty of autumn, we remember them.

In the beginning of the year and when it ends, we remember them.

When we are weary and in need of strength, we remember them.

When we are lost and sick at heart, we remember them.

When we have joys we yearn to share, we remember them. So long as we live, they too shall live, for they are now a part of us, as we remember them.

I believe I provided you with evidence that your loved ones are right here, next to us, watching Wheel of Fortune or in car rides with us as we drive to and from work—or in the serious moments when we feel doubt and need connection with them.

Those loved ones are with you when you cry at their grave; they're with you when you cry in the shower, or when you're in deep moments of grief as tears creep up in the corner of your eyes while boiling water for your kids' mac n cheese dinner. They hold the souls of your unborn child. They're with you when you hit milestones and when you're going through growing pains, telling you to slow down or "don't sweat the small stuff", or to buy the damn pick up truck—and spend time on vacation with your loved ones. Your loved ones are always there; this I promise you!

I've written the experiences in this book for you to hold them close and dear to your heart. I know the heartache after the loss of a loved one and how we have to learn how to navigate this world without them (here in person). We have to learn how to continue on, how to connect and communicate with their souls. You don't always need someone like me to do this for you and your loved ones in Heaven. Our loved ones choose us as their Heaven, because, why wouldn't they?

I Wrote This Book Because

I Wrote This Book for many reasons… I wanted to share how many of us were born with intuitive, psychic, and extra sensory gifts. Remember, if you hide them and suppress them over the years, you will develop anxiety or depression. Don't worry, suppressing them is quite common. But once you accept those gifts and learn to work with them, you realize they have always been there beneath the surface, waiting to be awakened. You might suffer the darkness alone and be labeled the black sheep of the family, or called crazy for assuming things that turn out to be true. That's your strong intuition and gifts of being an empath, psychic, or medium. Embrace them! Being a psychic medium is truly just an ability to read the soul of a human and the souls inside of heaven. I do not share my thoughts in this book with you because I think they will change the minds of people who think differently. I share my thoughts to show others who already think like me or experience things like me or have these gifts, that they are not alone.

I want you all to know that I can be your safe haven if you are in deep grief, searching for answers, or simply wanting to connect with your departed loved ones. With my abilities, I pretty much have the spare key to Heaven.

Also, if you're lost and scared of your gifts, oftentimes, for people like me, and especially people like my brother, there are multiple ways to seek help. Hearing, seeing, and feeling things not of this world does not necessarily mean you need a medical solution, but instead a spiritual one.

Remember, we are not human beings having a spiritual experience; we are spiritual beings having a human experience (Tielhard de Chardin). Please don't hesitate to reach out to me or Pat Longo, as she is someone I care for and trust.

I wrote this book to offer answers to those questions about what the inside of Heaven is like. I also wished to show how to navigate this world without those we love once they transition to the other side.

After every loss within your Soul Group, you will no doubt have a Spiritual awakening, and your loved ones are going to send you frequent signs from the other side. Don't think you're crazy. Be open. Talk about it. In some cultures, death is celebrated the same way a person's birthday is celebrated, as if a graduation from this life school here on Earth: a rebirth to the next life.

There is so much more to life than this world, so keep talking to your loved ones in Heaven, and ask them for signs, and please start journaling: start a dialogue with them; ask for specific signs! I promise you, they will show up and deliver. Talking to your angels and your past loved ones on the other side is normal. What makes me anxious is being part of a society that doesn't question the other side ever or that makes a person who does so seem abnormal. I think we need to question life daily and wonder why we are here; we must ask ourselves if we are fulfilling our life's paths and purposes. We're only here for a short time; we might as well make the most of that time. Normalize talking to your Angels, especially if you have small children, so that we can create a cycle of new experiences, for us and the next generation, surrounding our departed loved ones.

If you have a need to seek my spiritual services, don't be afraid. I take this work very seriously, and I treat it like a therapy session for the soul. I provide healing messages from the other side, and you do not have to be afraid. I won't tell you about a death, unless I can prevent it. I have surrendered fully to provide healing messages for the highest good of all concerned, and I look forward to our sessions together. Please feel free to reach out to me with any questions you have. You can contact me at www.aprilnatale.com.

Acknowledgements

I want to tell my children, Stephen and Mariah, I am so proud to be your mother, and I thank you for being a part of my spiritual journey here on Earth. You both were so loving and empathic towards me when Grandpa John and Gramma Honey crossed over. You hugged me; you wiped my tears away and whispered sweet nothings into my ear when I felt my world crashing down. I knew in those moments, I was raising you both so right. I know that, whatever I do in this life, being a mother will remain the greatest of gifts God has ever given me, a gift I would not trade for the world. I love you forever; remember to go within, during times of darkness, and to talk to your Angels: they will always lead the way.

Mom, I want to thank you for gently listening to me when I came out of the psychic closet with these experiences; pat yourself on the back for birthing such a gifted little child. I've been writing books to you since elementary school; I wanted to write this book for you during your most difficult time of grief. I thought maybe you'd make your way back to us. I have to honor the fact that, like many others, you might never be the same after losing the love of your life, and your beloved mother. Please be gentle with yourself. I love you. Remember, this pain is all part of the plan. We will get through this. I promise you that your hubby is always right next to you in the car rides and watching your nightly shows with you on the couch. Gramma Honey is there, telling you to take it easy on yourself, to make sure you zipper up your purse and keep it closed. Don't lose hope with Antonio; he will get the help he needs and the laws will change for persistent family members like us. Unfortunately his struggle is our new normal, but over time it won't sting anymore. We will continue to grow as a family and get through whatever life throws at us. Love you. #4

To all of my siblings: I wrote this book so our voices can be heard. At the same time, I wanted you all to understand me as your sister. I don't want to be misunderstood anymore: I put a lot of love and truth into the stories. We are all cut from the same cloth, yet so torn apart: I want us all to heal and stand by one another. How powerful we could be together if we could all just unite!

Most importantly, I wrote this for our struggling brother: Antonio, you are my brother and you really never caught a break in this life. You told me God told you I was the chosen one; I rolled my eyes at you, but now I believe you. I was constantly trying to save you and help you live out your full life's destiny. The last time I saw you in person, I told you "Don't go out to California." You calmly told me to trust you and that I was living in too much fear; I now believe you. I trust in some odd way that you and I are exactly where we are supposed to be—attempting to change this world and help people go through a massive spiritual shift. Now that I've written this book, it will end up opening a bigger platform to make our voices heard. I hope it will end up with someone who will help bring you back home to us. I miss you; you were always the one to say "I love you," so I'll continue to say "Ditto last! With lots of love, Your loving sister, April!"

(As I get ready to publish this book, I'd like to update all the readers so far as to how powerful your prayers are for my brother; they've been heard. He is currently receiving much needed healthcare and will be provided housing in an assisted living facility, with an outstanding medically trained staff, a program in California called the Ella's Foundation. I must add there is only one such facility in this country that cares for those with mental illness like my brother. Makes you wonder, It's as if he knew exactly where to end up.)

Pat Longo, I want to thank you and everyone that has ever supported you on your spiritual journey: a journey which has led you to release more lightworkers of the world! Thank you for your love, light, and healing—for listening to me cry and pour out my heart and soul to you, so that I could heal myself and continue to help others. Pat, you helped me through the darkness when I felt like I was doing this alone.

Thank you for not freaking me out, but for calmly saying to me, "Yep, that's normal," when I told you I hear, see, and feel things not of this world; thanks for explaining to me something my soul already knew: connection with Spirit, Angels, and loved ones waiting to awaken us once again.

 Without people like you, I don't know where I would be right now, honestly, maybe sitting in a psych ward, doped up on antipsychotics. You saved me; you help people for all the right reasons and are often that last glimmer of hope for so many. Naturally, this book is a tribute to teachers like you! You have to realize just how important you are to the world and how your help brought me back to the ones I love, at a time when I felt I no longer belonged in this world, because I was always living between two worlds, and for most of my life, I didn't know who to consult to embrace my gifts.

You are truly a Godsend healer and saviour to so many.

To my High School English Teacher, Mr. Strauss: It is your loving light that emanates throughout the world that will keep many souls thriving. You are the best teacher any child could have in this life and the next. I hope everything you desire comes back to you tenfold. When I said, some children go to school to learn, and yet others may go to school to be loved, it was your love that helped many like myself.

Thank you so much for all the love you shared and continue to share, and once again, I am forever grateful for all of your help and guidance, yet you expected nothing in return.

"A gift is pure when it is given from the heart to the right
person at the right time and at the right place, and when
we expect nothing in return"
– The Bhagavad Gita

Lastly, my loving step dad: you may not have been my biological father, but you sure proved to me that love is greater than blood: you are my soul dad. I want to thank you for all the Cubs games we went to together and all of the love and support you gave me since you came into my life at such a young age. I was abused and scared, and you were my protector, as well as my mother's knight in shining armour. You knew how to love, and I want to thank your mother for that. Thank you for being my guide in this life—and now a spirit guide in the afterlife. I hope this book is a fitting tribute to you!

I don't think I ever got the chance to thank you for my Prom Night, either; you always had my back. In the weeks leading up to prom, I was going to an adult store with a few of my friends, and, of course, you just so happened to be driving by on your way to dinner with a friend. You asked me the next day, what in the world was I doing in a place like that; I jokingly said I was picking up my prom date Mr. Stud, and I really was! Mr. Stud was a male blow up doll wearing a Speedo that I took to prom. Don't worry, he wasn't that inappropriate, so when I made prom court, I made sure to bust him out on the dance floor, so that everyone could get a good laugh!

Later that night at the hotel rooms, we partied until the morning sun rose, and you were just clocking into work when you were dispatched about underage teens wreaking havoc at the local hotels. I, of course, wasn't drinking or doing anything illegal: I was too afraid I was gonna get caught by you once again. So when you and the other local police officers came to look at the security tapes, the managers asked you if you recognized any of us local teenagers, specifically the girl running down the halls with a blow up doll! You said, "nope I don't recognize a soul!" You always and forever will have my back, so I thank you for that. That, or you were totally embarrassed you even knew me! I love you, and although we didn't really say that enough, we sure still continue to show love for one another. I'll be seeing you in the most familiar places. Until we meet again. Love Always, April

About April

April Natale is a nurse and psychic medium, who has been seeing Spirit since she was a child and suffered from anxiety for years because she didn't understand her gift.

She eventually got help from International spiritual healer, teacher, and author, Pat Longo, who taught her how to understand and use her gifts. Soon she was channeling and relaying healing messages from the other side to people across the U.S.and now works with clients across the globe.

April now does readings for clients to help them deal with their grief and communicate with their loved ones who have crossed over.

She lives in Chicago, Illinois, and you can reach her through her website at: aprilnatale.com

What this world needs is a little bit more spirituality!

XO April Natale

Connect With Me

Website: www.aprilnatale.com

Email at: info@aprilnatale.com

Phone: 847-261-4498

Follow Me on Social Media:

Facebook – https://www.facebook.com/AprillNatale

Instagram – https://www.instagram.com/aprillnatale

Twitter – https://AprilNatale/twitter.com

LinkedIn – https://www.linkedin.com/in/april-n-82586819a

References

Pat Longo, International Spiritual Healer, Teacher and
Author of "The Gifts Beneath Your Anxiety"
Email: Patlongo1111@gmail.com
http://patlongo.net/new/
516-433-5279

Anthony Mrocka, Psychic Medium
Anthonymrocka.com
Email: Assistant@anthonymrocka.com
973-907-0044

ellasfoundation.org

Domestic Violence Hotline, 1–800–799–7233

NAMI Helpline at 800-950-NAMI, or, in a crisis, text
"NAMI" to 741741

National Suicide Prevention Lifeline, 1-800-273-8255

Veterans Hotline, 1-800-273-8255

CPSIA information can be obtained
at www.ICGtesting.com
Printed in the USA
BVHW040954120821
614280BV00015B/300/J

9 781737 509202